Total Quality Management in Libraries

A Sourcebook

Rosanna M. O'Neil

Chief, Cataloging Department
The Pennsylvania State University

1994
LIBRARIES UNLIMITED, INC.
Englewood, Colorado

LIBRARIES UNLIMITED, INC.
P.O. Box 6633
Englewood, CO 80155-6633
1-800-237-6124

Project Editor: Louisa M. Griffin
Design and Layout: Pamela J. Getchell
Proofreader: Laura Taylor

Library of Congress Cataloging-in-Publication Data

O'Neil, Rosanna M., 1957-
    Total quality management in libraries : a sourcebook / Rosanna M.
O'Neil.
    xvii, 194 p. 17x25 cm.
    Includes bibliographical references and index.
    ISBN 1-56308-247-0
    1. Library administration--United States. 2. Total quality
management. I. Title.
Z678.054 1994
025.1'0973--dc20   94-8011
                                                              CIP

Contents

Part I: TQM in Libraries: The Articles

Part II: Quality Management in Libraries: A Select Bibliography

Acknowledgments

Residing in central Pennsylvania without an adjacent library school made the compilation of this sourcebook quite a challenge. I would have been unable to complete it without the persistence of Penn State's interlibrary loan department, and in particular Noelene Martin, Ruth Senior, Barbara Coopey, and Mark Leskovansky. I am eternally grateful to all of them for their assistance and willingness to go far beyond the call of duty to make this book a reality.

My good friends, Leslie Pearse and Kathy Kie at OCLC, also rose to the occasion as I found titles at the last minute that the OCLC Corporate Library happened to own and which they quickly faxed off to me. Thanks also to Mary Kay Biagini at my alma mater, the University of Pittsburgh School of Library and Information Science, who rushed to my assistance and faxed me one of the articles reprinted here whose last several lines were not clear enough for the reprint. And a good friend of mine, Andrea Leyko, training librarian, who copied and faxed a last minute entry for my bibliography in record time.

Kim Colpetzer, Amy Maney, and Sondra Armstrong in the Information Access Services Division offered invaluable support throughout the months of this project. Amy Maney keyed in one of the articles, as did Billie Hackney, one of my copy cataloging supervisors (and both great typists). But in particular, my secretary, Kim, (even at 120 words per minute) tirelessly keyed in the majority of the reprinted articles until the words started to blur. She also photocopied many articles for my review and filed numerous interlibrary loan requests. She provided constant encouragement and prodding and I am fortunate to have someone like her to take care of me.

The Pennsylvania State University Libraries provides exceptional support for the research of its library faculty. This book would not have been possible without that support and I am proud to be a part of an institution that believes so strongly in the research and development of its librarians.

Finally, I must thank my husband, Phil Bankes, for his inpenetrable understanding. He has more patience than I deserve, yet even these months of late nights at the office were a challenge for him. Finding many a fine dinner waiting for me and an understanding greeting at the door were the support that propelled me to the end of this project. And it is for, and because of, this man of "quality" that this book has been compiled.

Introduction

The challenge is to view every element of every operation through a customer's lens; to constantly attempt to—literally—redefine each element of the business in terms of the customer's perceptions of the intangibles.

Tom Peters
Thriving on Chaos

While post-World War II United States manufacturers and the U.S. government were busy repatriating their soldiers into the workforce, the Japanese were rebuilding a country. Being a patient and methodical nation, it is no surprise that during the 1950s the Japanese embraced the data-driven, systems-focused approach of Americans W. Edwards Deming and Joseph Juran. By the time these two quality masters had succeeded in leading the Japanese to a new level of quality and customer service—enabling the Japanese to successfully infiltrate the U.S. marketplace—U.S. manufacturers were still wondering what hit them. The U.S. reaction to this discomfort was to start a campaign of "Buy American" while doing little to address the real issues of cost, quality, and customer service.

Discovering that patriotism was not going to keep them in business, U.S. manufacturers visited Japan to assess the rejuvenation of Japanese manufacturing promulgated by Deming and Juran. Much of the organizational dynamics they saw had also been slowly explored, tested, and employed on our own soil, but with two fundamental missing elements: 1) folding these efforts into the strategic direction of the organization, and 2) focusing on the external customer.

Going back to the early 1900s, Frederick Taylor's scientific management theories were the most prevalent in the United States. He believed that the only way to make employees do an honest day's work was to exercise strict control over the operation *and* the employees. The Industrial Engineering methods of measurement and standards were employed approximately 30 years later and focused on setting quotas and goals of production for workers. During World War II, fear caused America to address the issue of quality (reliable bombs and planes were always good to have during times of war), but the quality effort was based on one of multiple quality control checkpoints, not doing it right the first time. It didn't do much for organizational excellence, but it did help us win the war.

In the meantime, another type of war had begun and the prize was financial success. Enter just-in-time scheduling (also called just-in-time manufacturing), a Japanese productivity tool usually employed with other quality initiatives. The Japanese utilized just-in-time scheduling as one successful approach to organizational excellence, but for them it was a component fix and not the entire solution. Unfortunately, U.S. manufacturers used it as *the* solution to their problems. While it focused on getting rid of waste, the U.S. application was still focused inward, not outward toward the customer. And as they discovered, just-in-time didn't necessarily mean "just right."

Total quality management (TQM) brings together the best aspects of organizational excellence by driving out fear, offering customer-driven products and services, doing it right the first time by eliminating error, maintaining inventory control without waste, focusing on employee development and empowerment, and more, and completes it with strategic direction and a customer-driven culture.

TQM Defined

There are many well-phrased definitions of total quality management to be found in the literature of all industries, including our own. Rather than come up with some paraphrased version of the existing ones, I will share with you my favorite. It comes from *Corporate Dandelions* by Craig J. Cantoni.

> Some practitioners define TQM as conformance to customer requirements. Some define it by such analytical tools as histograms, fishbone diagrams, and statistical process/quality control charts. Others define it by the continuous improvement of key business processes. Still others define it by an organization-wide culture that reinforces quality in everything that it does.
>
> This book selects "all of the above" as the right definition ... TQM is a nonhierarchical and nonbureaucratic culture, based on an operating philosophy of employee involvement, committed to meeting customer requirements through the continuous improvement of key business processes, as measured by a variety of analytical tools.[1]

Obviously, memorizing the definition is not enough. Becoming familiar with the terminology is useful. And, reading more about the process, going through a good training program, and beginning to apply the practices, such as well-facilitated brainstorming, benchmarking, and data collection, is critical to becoming an active partner in changing the culture of the organization, and truly assessing and meeting the needs of your customers. This book is meant to support your efforts by providing you with some of the best articles from our own literature (where quality principles were actually applied or thought about for libraries). It comprises a fairly comprehensive bibliography of what has been published in this area (including tangential interests such as focus groups, leadership, and the "learning organization"); a glossary of total quality; and a list of resources to build your own in-house working collection for you and your staff as well as to facilitate further exploration of TQM.

Total Quality in Library Literature

The literature of total quality management in libraries is exploding before our eyes. Just during the six-month period between July 1993 and December 1993, more than 30 individual offerings have either been indexed or have appeared in library literature. Oddly enough, being involved in total quality management at the Pennsylvania State University for over two years now, I find myself in the lull after the storm. It has become a part of our lives at the university and a part of me and how I think and evaluate all situations. I keep up with its ebbs and flows in business, industry, education, and libraries, as I would other topics of my profession. I believe you, too, will hit that comfortable lull after the storm as the culture in your library slowly changes from defensiveness to openness, from tunnel vision to systems thinking, from "gut" feeling decisions to data-driven improvements, and from quality thoughts to quality actions.

While I have always been the type to question *ad nauseam* (to the chagrin of many!), that's what TQM does, in a sense. But it brings with it a structure for this constant state of query: of wanting to do the best, be the best, and seek the best practices. It causes a mind set that is one of process focus with people initiatives, of pointing out process faults not people faults, of the joy of winning together rather than winning alone, of customer-driven products based on customer input, and of putting the best foot forward and making sure your shoes are shined.

Quality in Libraries

Based upon the number of articles already published in library literature, it would appear that libraries have been, and are increasingly embracing the theories, philosophies, and practices of total quality management. Some might say that we've always cared about good service and quality products, so why embrace this new approach? Here are some possible reasons:

- The organization in which we reside has mandated it.

- Times are getting tougher and we need to prove our worth more than ever before (and get our customers on our side and verbalizing their support).

- There are many advocates of the process, both in our profession and others, and they've convinced us to at least give it a chance.

- We've seen successes in business and industry and see the parallels (although some loathe to admit it).

- We've come to realize that the world of knowledge and the potential for acquisition and access is so dramatic, and perhaps overwhelming, that we actually *need* customer input to make the best decisions.

- We see TQM as a useful and effective vehicle for change (not only of others and processes, but of ourselves).

How Well Do We Know Our Customers?

In my total quality experiences so far, I believe that the most difficult pill to swallow has been the possibility that we don't actually know what the customer wants. Heresy to think that our gut feelings aren't right on the mark; that the surveys we've conducted are nothing more than asking patrons (our customers) to say whether or not we're doing a good job in their eyes, but not asking them what they might have needed but didn't get, or what we could be doing better; and that because we have high circulation statistics, that what we're offering is either what they wanted, needed, or even came to the library for, and, that the experience was a good one. Let's say, for example, a patron looked in our wonderful online catalog and asked for directions to the stack area (and was treated like a fool for not knowing—I've actually witnessed this treatment); got to the right point in the maze and couldn't find the book; went to Circulation and waited in line (let's say, three to five minutes—an eternity to them); discovered the book hadn't been reshelved yet (after waiting for someone to go behind the scenes and figure that out); tried to check the book out, but found he or she needed to register first and had to fill out a form (not a big deal, but at this point!); and left merrily(?) with book in hand. Is that good service? After you've answered that question (objectively), try these:

- Do customers expect adequate, good, or excellent service?

- Do products and services meet the needs of the customers? Do we really know what those needs are, real or perceived?

- Do we have the *right* people in the *right* positions to provide the customer with services they want?

- Do we always have an excuse for *why* we don't provide a service, rather than investigate the validity of the request?

- Do we listen to the frontline workers and act on their feedback?

- Do we make *assumptions* of our customers' needs and provide services which reflect those biases?

- Is the online catalog effective in guiding the user to the proper materials? And how have we helped the patron to discern what the *proper* materials are?

- Do we benchmark with (i.e., compare with and aspire to) the best collections and services in our profession? With our competitors?

- Are we willing to admit that as aprofession we are providing a service and that this isn't such a bad thing?

- Can we accept that the provision of information doesn't lie solely with libraries today and that we indeed have competitors that are eating us alive with quick turnarounds and quality service?

- Do we lie low and let vendors define what we need in libraries or are we active partners in the design process?

- When we make changes in our workflow, do we ask customers (internal and external) how this might affect them? Do we *pilot* changes or simply implement them?

- Do we deal with poor performers in order to motivate good performers and to ensure quality services to the customer?

- Do we treat colleagues and patrons with trust and respect?

- Do we actively participate in ALA, SLA, MLA, ARL, or other professional societies, to ensure continual learning?[2]

Not every one of these questions has to go through a nine-month structured evaluation. However, in a customer-driven organization it is not assumed that one automatically has the answers based on years of experience. The key is to not just go about one's work in the same old way. For example, let's take something as simple as a new flyer designed for internal use. Instead of sending out a memo describing this new communication vehicle (some don't even do that), in a TQM culture one would consider a beta test of the flyer and ask for feedback (ask for customer reaction and input). The flyer would be crafted so that it was truly clear and therefore useful from everyone's vantage point (do it right the first time) based on customer input and feedback. And then, it would be revisited a few years later and the customer queried again for possible improvements (continuous improvement). All in the spirit of a culture which is geared toward an ongoing, continuous improvement process that is satisfying, rewarding, empowering up and down the line, and, above all, customer driven.

Changing the Library Culture

As a cataloger I am told much too often that the patron never reads the record. They just want the call number so they can find the item. In a traditional library environment, the reaction of the cataloging department is one of defensiveness, defending this finely tailored product over which we (or some other library) have slaved just for the patrons because *we know* they need this information.

It is for some threatening and quite unpleasant to allow those outside our units to criticize our work. Frankly, how can anyone know better than us how to do our jobs and do them well? But, criticism of the usefulness of the catalog record (mentioned above) remains as criticism if not used as an opportunity for improvement. After all, they are our customers speaking and our time-honored excuses should no longer be used to allow us to do our jobs "the same old way." I recently read somewhere that we should rate our customer service orientation by how we respond to complaints. If we provide excuses, we're not listening. If we use those complaints as opportunities for introspection and for improvement, we are truly customer driven. Let's try the complaint above as an example. Let's pass this question through the "five whys" process.[3] This process is used when one is unsure of the root cause of a problem. For example:

> **Problem:** According to the Reference staff, patrons don't read the record.
>
> **Why?** The OPAC screen isn't clear.
>
> **Why?** They only want the location so they can check the item out or photocopy an article.
>
> **Why?** There's a lot of superfluous and muddy information based on preconceived notions of what patrons must have to recognize a unique bibliographic entity so they ignore the rest of the record.
>
> **Why?** The Reference staff is uncomfortable with the record and believes that patrons are as well.
>
> **Why?** The call number placement encourages patrons to ignore the rest of the information.
>
> **Why?** The user education classes don't explain the record to patrons in such a way that they appreciate the wealth of information there and its possible usefulness.

The idea is to come up with a minimum of five whys; I gave six and could come up with more! The point is you have to be willing to admit that you don't have all of the answers; that customer ideas should not be criticized, but rather used as opportunities for improvement; that there is indeed accountability for every service we provide; and that together, in a systems-thinking environment, we can try our best and go beyond to be innovative and creative in our problem-solving techniques (a total quality approach) and to share ideas and enthusiasm for change. Recently, I came across an advertisement in *USA Today* for 3M that depicts the company as an "innovative" organization. According to the ad, the company offers "an atmosphere that encourages creative initiative, a policy of reaching beyond without fear of failure, a way of looking at separate technologies, that invites the cross-fertilization of ideas." [4]

What needs to be accepted in our profession is that the answers are no longer simple, and that our institutions are demanding accountability for their financial support, not gut feelings. Total quality management practices are a time-tested, data-driven means of either proving our gut feelings to be accurate, or forcing us to accept that they are not. And it enables us to focus on making the necessary changes for providing quality products and services to our customers who can now go elsewhere for information more often and more easily than ever before.

I hope that some of the successes reprinted here, along with further readings from the bibliography and training in total quality practices will set you on a course towards a culture of total quality and of continuous improvement. The initial start-up can be slow as all are trained and the culture slowly shifts, but the breakthroughs along the way, the quick fixes that show immediate results, and more satisfied customers, make it worth the effort to begin the quality journey.

How to Use This Book

This book is meant to be a reference work, as well as a source of information on total quality management for libraries. It is by no means a comprehensive tool for implementing TQM in your setting.

In the earlier part of this introduction, you were given a brief history and definition of TQM, and were offered some food for thought on TQM and libraries.

The majority of this book is comprised of reprinted articles from the library literature from the early 1980s through 1994. The contributions have been selected to provide an A-to-Z overview and to exhibit some practical applications in libraries. That section also includes one original and timely article on customer focus written by Barbara Armstrong, the national quality manager of the National Information Resource Centre at Telecom Australia.

The annotated bibliography that follows is intended to bring together a fairly comprehensive listing of the contributions to our literature to date and to assist you in selecting further reading.

The appendixes are a mixture of additional resources for your TQM journey. They include a suggested working collection (including titles to add to the general circulating collection), publications to monitor for continuous learning, associations/publishers involved in TQM, training opportunities if training in total quality is not available at your institution, awards presented in the area of total quality management, and how to access TQM information and discussions on the electronic information highway.

The glossary provides definitions for terms found in both the reprints and the bibliography, as well as a working glossary for your own TQM applications.

To supplement this work as the literature on quality continues to enrich our profession, I will be setting up a file on the Pennsylvania State University Libraries' Gopher to which I will continue to add entries (books and articles from the library literature or by librarians), briefly annotated. You may contact me at:

Rosanna O'Neil
Chief, Cataloging Department
The Pennsylvania State University
E506 Pattee Library
University Park, PA 16802
Tel.: (814) 865-1755
Fax: (814) 863-7293
E-mail: rmo@psulias.psu.edu
        rmo@psulias.bitnet

I hope this work will be of ongoing use in your quest for total quality in your library.

Notes

1. Craig J. Cantoni, *Corporate Dandelions*. New York: Amacom, 1993.

2. Barbara Spiegelman, "Total Quality Management in Libraries," in *Library Management Quarterly* 16, no. 3 (Summer 1992): 12-16. (Based on quality audit questions.)

3. *Tools and Techniques for Continuous Improvement: Pocket Guide.* Wilmington, Del.: DuPont Corporate Quality Resource Center, 1993.

4. 3M advertisement, *USA Today*, 24 January 1994, 12C.

PART I
TQM in Libraries:
The Articles

Total Quality Management: Customer-Centered Models for Libraries

Susan B. Barnard

Kent State University Libraries, ARL/OMS Visiting Program Officer

Conduct a keyword search on "quality" in a research library's online catalog and you're likely to have hundreds of hits. An ever-growing body of literature, dating from the 1960s forward, documents American business' conversion to such management concepts as "quality circles," "quality assurance," "quality control" and others—all aimed at improving U.S. products, services, productivity, and competitiveness in the world market. Perhaps the most comprehensive and pervasive term in the quality lexicon today is "total quality management" or TQM.

Total quality management combines theories, tools, and organizational models developed in Japanese, European, and U.S. industry during the past several decades. Simply defined, TQM is "a system of continuous improvement centered on the needs of customers." Hallmarks of TQM include employee involvement at all levels; commitment to employee training and development; the use of problem-solving teams, quality control standards and statistical methods; long-term (instead of short-term) goals and thinking; and recognition that the system (not employees) is responsible for most inefficiencies.

A current initiative of ARL's Office of Management Services (OMS) is to evaluate the potential of a total quality management approach for improving service and effectiveness in research libraries. One objective of the OMS project is to develop a training program for research library managers and staff who wish to consider implementing TQM in their libraries. A brief look at the development of TQM in the U.S., and an explanation of its key concepts may suggest how TQM can be applied in research libraries.

TQM in the U.S.

Total quality management and, in fact, what has been called a "quality revolution" in American management during the past 20 to 30 years, are traceable to the principles advanced by Dr. W. Edwards Deming, an American statistician and management theorist. Deming's landmark

(Reprinted with permission of the Association of Research Libraries.)

work with Japanese manufacturers following World War II is credited with helping Japan to dramatically improve the quality of its products and thereby regain its world economic position. Deming's principles, summarized in his fourteen points for management, have been adopted by hundreds of U.S. companies, including Ford Motor Company, Xerox, Hewlett-Packard, and Motorola. A 1990 survey found that about 50 percent of *Business Week*'s 1000 top companies had initiated a quality improvement program of some type.

Firmly established in business and industry, TQM is now being embraced in government, the military, education, and other non-profit sectors. The Federal Quality Institute in Washington, D.C. was established in 1988 to promote and facilitate the implementation of TQM throughout the federal government. In higher education, Oregon State University has been a pioneer in adapting TQM to the university environment. In its TQM implementation process, OSU formed ten pilot problem-solving teams to work in various areas of its Finance and Administration division, including business affairs, physical plant, human resources, and computing services. Recently, OSU has begun to employ TQM in academic areas, including the library. A survey conducted by OSU in 1990 showed that at least 25 other universities, including Harvard, Carnegie-Mellon, and the Universities of Chicago, Michigan, Minnesota, North Carolina, and Wisconsin, were involved with the TQM process or had implemented TQM programs in some areas of operation.[1]

"Quality," "Management," and "Customers" in the TQM Context

Like any comprehensive operational model, TQM employs specialized terminology which may sound like jargon to the uninitiated. Academics, in particular, may be suspicious of what can appear to be the latest business fad, inappropriate for the teaching and research environment of a university. An understanding of the meanings of the key TQM concepts of "quality," "management," and "customers" is essential to a fuller consideration of the potential of TQM in any setting.

In the manufacturing sector where the concept of quality control originated, "quality" was defined in terms of conformance to fixed product specifications. Similarly, in libraries one measure of quality is conformance to national standards, such as those used in cataloging and authority control. However, within TQM, quality is not defined according to absolute standards but more relatively, in terms of customer need. One definition says that "the quality of service is defined by the customer's perception of both the quality of the product and the service providing it." Moreover, there has been a shift from simply meeting customer expectations and requirements to anticipating and exceeding the ever-changing needs of customers, who may not even express or be aware of their needs. Some TQM enthusiasts sum it up by saying that quality is "delighting the customer."

In total quality management "customers" are, broadly defined, "the beneficiaries of a company's (or an organization's) work." Further, in TQM there are both external customers and internal customers, and these may be people or organizations.[2] External customers are beneficiaries outside of the organization—whether profit or non-profit—namely, customers, clients, patients, constituents, patrons, users, etc. Internal customers, or beneficiaries within an organization, may be in the next office, another department or another division of the organization. Thus, faculty are internal customers in a university, though from the library's perspective they may be external customers, too. Similarly, library reference personnel may be viewed as internal customers for those in acquisitions, cataloging, or circulation, and vice versa. This is particularly applicable with regard to mutual support functions which enable staff to do their jobs and provide service to users more effectively. The Deming directive to "break down barriers between departments" is a fundamental objective of TQM which is facilitated by the concept of internal customers.

While the commitment of management at all levels is critical to the success of TQM in an organization, TQM is not strictly, or simply, a management tool. The role of management in TQM changes from giving directions to that of empowering the people who run the processes, deliver the services, and otherwise do the work at all levels. It emphasizes leadership over management and requires significant conceptual change by managers and all other employees in the way they view their roles in the organization.

TQM and Research Libraries

Can TQM, a system designed for and successfully applied in business and manufacturing settings, be effectively employed in non-profit, service organizations such as libraries? Deming says his principles apply to any business, education, or government, wherever an organization must stay ahead of its customers. TQM embodies certain values and approaches common to research libraries today, suggesting that libraries may already be engaging in TQM-type initiatives without calling them that.

For example, TQM promotes employee training and development as a way to improve an organization's performance, ability to respond to changing customer demands, and involvement of employees at all levels. Likewise, libraries recognize the importance of investing in and developing staff to improve individual and organizational effectiveness and flexibility. Libraries are also employing participative management methods to increase staff involvement and distribute decision-making more widely. Interdepartmental committees and councils are well-established in libraries, and a few pioneer libraries are experimenting with teams and self-managing work groups.

Another essential element of TQM and Dr. Deming's principles is the reliance upon "statistical methods" to gather and analyze data about the processes of production and operation and to continuously improve these processes. In libraries, there is a growing emphasis on the development and application of valid performance measures for assessing productivity, efficiency, and service effectiveness. Academic libraries are joining public libraries in utilizing marketing techniques, such as user surveys and focus groups, to obtain feedback from users and formulate or improve program objectives. Universities as well are turning to various methods of outcomes assessment to evaluate the effectiveness of specific programs and overall perfor-mance, as well as to substantiate requests for resources.

These and other concepts are fundamental to TQM. Yet, TQM is more than the sum of its parts, a checklist of strategies and initiatives to be applied. TQM is said to effectuate "cultural transformation" within organizations and, thus, may have the potential to combine and expand upon familiar concepts to create new paradigms of library operation and organization.

Transformation comes from many directions and cannot be accomplished quickly, cheaply, or easily. Among the most powerful TQM-inspired shifts for libraries could be the reconceptualizing of library users as customers, library staff as internal customers, and all that these changes imply. Libraries have a long-standing claim to being service-oriented, but good service practices have traditionally been defined within the library pro-fession from its own knowledge base and operational experience, rather than by the consumers of library products and services. While professional knowl-edge, standards, and codes which have been developed over decades cannot be disregarded or summarily thrown aside, it would probably benefit librari-anship, and other professions as well, to create ongoing dialogue with our customers for the purpose of better understanding and anticipating their information needs. We may find that there is less similarity between service-orientation and customer-centeredness than we think.

The potential for TQM to bring about organizational transformation in research libraries could be less dramatic than that which it has fostered in factories and other business environments. However, despite steps toward participative management and other innovations, the organiza-tional structure of research libraries today typically remains hierarchical. Total quality management suggests and can lead to the development of an alternative organizational model for libraries which can enable them to be more flexible, responsive, and proactive within a milieu where the only certainty seems to be rapid, nonstop change.

References

1. Coate, L. Edwin. *Implementing Total Quality Management in a Uni-versity Setting*. Oregon State University, July 1990.

2. Glenn, Tom. "The Formula for Success in TQM," *The Bureaucrat: Journal for Public Managers*. Spring 1991, pp. 17-20.

TQM: Quality Improvement in New Clothes

Donald E. Riggs

*University Library, University of Michigan,
Ann Arbor, Michigan*

The total quality management (TQM) movement is alive and thriving throughout the Fortune 1000 firms, the federal government, city governments, hotels, and even in our local hospitals. It is spreading across America like a new religion. And it is moving quickly into the academy. The range of TQM implementation in higher education extends from our most prestigious universities to community colleges.

W. Edwards Deming, an American statistician whose ideas about quality found little favorable response at home, lectured in 1950 to the Japanese. He excoriated them for their cheap, shoddy goods and told them that an emphasis on quality would result in lasting benefits in market share and profitability. He laid out principles for making quality a strategic advantage. They listened to him. They also listened to Joseph Juran in 1954, and later to Philip Crosby.[1] The Japanese struggled with adapting the quality principles, and they pursued the quality ideal relentlessly. The rest, as they say, is history. Hard-pressed American firms began the quality improvement process in the early 1980s. Quality became Job 1 in many companies (e.g., IBM, Ford, Motorola), and the U.S. Navy coined the phrase *total quality management.*

Simply put, libraries are a natural entity for TQM. Is there any library not pursuing improvement in its service? To take this line of thinking a step further, most libraries are pursuing excellence in their products and services. We do not hear library staff saying, "We are committed to mediocrity around here." Libraries are essentially service organizations, and nearly all people working in academic libraries want to offer the very best service to the students and faculty. Users (consumers) describe quality by the characteristics of the product or service they acquire: it is available, it is exactly the information being sought, service is good, and library staff is courteous and helpful. Quality is what one needs and wants, not what you think is needed or what is convenient for you to deliver. To paraphrase Peter Drucker, "Libraries do not exist for people who work in them, but for the people they serve." TQM advocates not only meeting the users' needs but also anticipating and exceeding the ever-changing needs of users. The academic library's users are normally thought of as being primarily the students and faculty. However, the library construct has its own internal users (e.g., the public services' staff are users of the products processed by the technical services' staff).

Ideally, before a library begins rolling out TQM, a strategic plan is in place. The principles of TQM frequently refer back to the library's mission and vision statements, goals, objectives, and strategies. A strategic plan provides focus and articulation to the library's multiyear expectations. The strategies formulated to advance the library must reflect the best thinking available, and they most certainly have to include action steps to be followed by specific library personnel. Like commitment to strategic planning, TQM requires that the library's top management, by word and deed, display commitment to continuous quality improvement. TQM has to be entrenched in the rhetoric of the library's leadership; resources allocation/redeployment is necessary to make "walk the talk" evident.

Most importantly, the quest for quality must be given meaning through actions.[2] Advocates of TQM call for more than a change in management practices. They want an entirely new organization, one whose culture is quality-driven, customer-oriented, marked by teamwork, and avid about improvement.

Since libraries are already user-focused and practice continuous improvement, how is TQM different from what is currently being done? Notable principles of TQM are embodied in the following areas:

- **Managing by fact**. Many library decisions are made without a careful analysis of the facts. Objective data are of prime importance in TQM decision making. Such an approach reduces debate about opinions. Measurement within the context of the library's TQM is feedback for improvement. Accompanying the measurement process is systematic problem solving. Root causes of the problem are identified and a cause-and-effect analysis is done for the specific problem. Checksheets, histograms, and Pareto charts are examples of tools used during the analysis.

- **Eliminating rework**. Much of the work done in academic/research libraries is labor-intensive. The trick is to simplify the work and make certain it is done right the first time. The time spent fixing earlier mistakes is useless and expensive. The rework can equal as much as 20 percent of all operating costs in a library.

- **Respecting people and ideas**. TQM aims at developing teamwork throughout the library. And the library's most valuable resource is its staff. In most library work situations, the people who know what really is needed to improve users' services are those who are working directly with the user. However, many times they are reluctant to bring the problem issues to the attention of their supervisors. These staff members should be encouraged to express their ideas on how service can be improved. And if criticism is necessary, their ideas, not the staff members, should be challenged. Staff should be encouraged to point out problems without fearing they will be held responsible. Management by fear cannot be tolerated in a continuous improvement environment.

- **Empowering people**. TQM empowers people by trusting all library staff to act responsibly and giving them proper authority. Generally speaking, library staff want to do the right and better thing. Barriers have to be removed in order for the staff to improve the processes. In Deming's view, 85 percent of all problems are traceable to the process itself, and just 15 percent to the people. He admonishes managers to stop attacking the people and begin attacking the process.[3] Unquestionably, decision making needs to be made at the lowest possible level in a TQM library, and such a library will probably become a flatter organization.

TQM is not an entirely new management technique for libraries. It does, however, offer a more formal, systematic approach to focusing on continuous improvement. The customer/user is TQM's centerpiece. One should not expect TQM to solve all problems nor should it be viewed as a quick fix. Organizations that have failed in their TQM endeavor have tried to implement it too quickly without proper staff training. An effective TQM process is gradually implemented in a library over a two- to three-year period. And it will require a commitment of resources, especially for the intensive training.

Is TQM just another management fad (Or, as the Chinese say, a gust of wind)? Based on the recent incline of quality throughout our society, the quality movement is here to stay. And who can argue with the improvement of quality in libraries?

References

1. Ted Marchese, "TQM Reaches the Academy," *AAHE Bulletin* 44:3-9 (Nov. 1991).

2. Daniel T. Seymour, *On Q: Causing Quality in Higher Education* (New York: Macmillan, 1992).

3. W. Edwards Deming, *Out of the Crisis* (Cambridge, Mass.: MIT Center for Advanced Engineering Study, 1985).

Think Quality! The Deming Approach Does Work in Libraries

Terry Mackey and Kitty Mackey

Terry Mackey is Reference Coordinator, University of South Carolina at Spartanburg and Kitty Mackey is Head of Public Services, Converse College, Spartanburg, South Carolina.

A student came to the reference desk and asked the reference librarian for help with a paper on Ecuador.

The librarian, Brooke, smiled and said, "Ecuador?"

"Yes, Ecuador."

"Okay let me show you the *Readers' Guide*."

An hour later, after the shift change, the student came back to the reference desk and asked another reference librarian, Leslie, "for help with a paper on Ecuador." Leslie smiled and asked, "What class is this for?" The student explained that it was for an international marketing project and indicated where "the other librarian" had taken her for information. Leslie once again smiled, and after she had finished explaining *Business Periodicals Index*, the *Wall Street Journal Index*, and other business reference sources, charged back to the head of Public Services.

"I just helped a frustrated student with the research for a major paper in international marketing. One of our librarians helped her earlier but only took her to the *Readers' Guide*, which did no good! This is really a problem. It keeps happening over and over. The student was upset, and I don't blame her. We caused her to waste at least an hour looking in the wrong place. What are we going to do?"

What this library staff could do is adopt the Deming Total Quality Management (TQM) method to address their obvious problems in attaining quality service. W. Edwards Deming's method is a big buzzword around big business these days—many corporate libraries may even be part of a TQM program adopting the principles of Deming or other quality gurus like J. M. Juran and Philip Crosby—but all libraries can benefit from building quality into the job process, whether it is reference service as above, online cataloging, staff training, etc. These philosophies are totally antithetical to the often-cited management by objectives (MBO) philosophy, which emphasizes results over process.

Four decades ago, the American Deming, the "father of the quality revolution," helped the Japanese become the world manufacturing leaders they are today, and U.S. manufacturers are only just not catching up. U.S. service industries (of which libraries are one) have been reluctant to adopt this philosophy—saying "service is different than manufacturing"—but more are doing so, as highlighted in a special bonus issue of *Business Week*, October 25, 1991.

The real reason most service managers don't adopt Deming may be that they are so busy fighting fires they don't have time to reflect. We hope this article, translating Deming's concepts into the language of libraries, provides that opportunity and guidance.

Adoption of the Deming philosophy begins with an understanding of his "14 Points." In *Out of Crisis* (MIT Pr., 1986 and the source for his quotes hereafter, unless otherwise cited), Deming introduces his 14 points:

> It will not suffice merely to solve problems, big or little. Adoption and action on the 14 points are a signal that management intends to stay in business and aims to protect investors and jobs. Such a system formed the basis for lessons for top management in Japan in 1950 and in subsequent years. The 14 points apply anywhere, to small organizations as well as to large ones, to the service industry as well as to manufacturing.

That said, here they are.

The 14 Points

Point 1. Create Constancy of Purpose for Improvement of Product and Service

Deming observed that there are two kinds of problems—those of today and those of tomorrow. He accurately states that it "is easy to stay bound up in the tangled knot of problems of today, becoming ever more and more efficient in them."

In the library, constancy of purpose is embodied in its mission statement, but it is easy to forget that the mission statement was created to help cope with both kinds of problems. It is also easy to forget that the mission statement exists and thus begin to make decisions independent of it, something akin to the Supreme Court making decisions without consulting the Constitution.

Without a mission statement, understood by everyone and consulted regularly, a library cannot maintain constancy of purpose. If consulting the mission statement is always the first step, then polling the library users must be the second. To operate without asking what the user needs is to be self-serving.

Point 2. Adopt the New Philosophy

The pursuit of quality must become the primary motivation of everyone in the organization. Mary Walton in *The Deming Management Method* (Perigee: Putnam, 1986) describes this pursuit as "adopting the new religion." The idea is to leap from measuring results to measuring the process by which the results are achieved.

For example, research questions answered by the reference staff could increase from 500 the previous semester to 720, but while increase—as an end result—would look impressive on the annual report, it reveals nothing about the quality of the answers given. If the extra 220 answers were all incorrect, was service improved? No. All the totals show is that the staff gave *more* service, not *better* service. If, however, the process by which the service was delivered is examined, there is opportunity to say confidently that service was improved. The question is not "How many?" but rather "How?"

Several information-charting techniques—such as flow charting—are useful at this juncture. The figure below illustrates a condensed flow chart of the reference process that the authors employed in conjunction with a user survey. Note how each question corresponds to a specific juncture in the reference process. This enabled the reference staff to pinpoint specific problems and isolate weaknesses in the process.

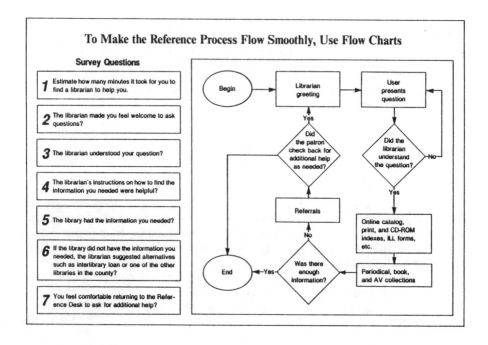

Flow-charting a process is not enough. Building quality into the process requires an understanding of statistics that reveal how common-cause and special-cause variations are at work. Common-cause variations will cause minor fluctuations in a stable process while special-cause variations create the peaks and valleys that catch the eye. Special-cause variations need to be remedied; common-cause variations may need to be remedied, but only when the variation falls outside the established parameters of quality. Without charting the process over time it is difficult to distinguish common variations from special variations.

Another form of variation, tampering, must also be controlled. Tampering is that tendency to "fix things" even before it is established that there is indeed something to fix.

Other tools for graphically representing a process include:

- **Run charts**, which plot information over a period of time. Something to plot on a run chart would be the number of interlibrary loan (ILL) transactions handled each week over an academic year, for instance.

- **Control charts**, which take run charts a step further by adding parameters to the chart, a baseline, an upper control limit, and a lower control limit. For example, in charting turnaround time for ILL transactions, it may be established that seven days is the baseline or average, three days is the lower control limit, and ten days is the upper control limit. ILL transactions could then be plotted on the chart and the process studied to identify common-cause variations and special-cause variations.

- **Pareto charts**, which are used to measure several variables, such as types of questions answered at the reference desk. Walton points out that pareto charts are sometimes described as a way to sort out the "vital few" from the "trivial many."

- **Fishbone cause—and—effect charts**, which are very useful for analyzing complex processes, particularly where several people are involved, and often serve as the outline for a brainstorming session. The fishbone chart usually divides a process into four input categories: materials, methods, manpower, and machines.

Once an entire process has been charted it is easier to see where changes may be added to improve the output—quality. Even number-phobes will be converted to statistical processes when they see the gains.

Point 3. Cease Dependence on Mass Inspection to Achieve Quality

Mass inspection is a result-oriented attitude and therefore not conducive to producing quality. "Quality," says Deming (as quoted in Walton's book), "comes not from inspection but from improvement of the process. The old way: Inspect bad quality out . The new way: Build good quality in."

Deming's philosophy builds quality into every step of the process. If errors occur, find out where and why and adjust the process, not the people. Deming assumes that people want to take pride in their work and will do quality work if they are given the opportunity. Listening to employee comments and facilitating their suggestions must be management's top priority.

For instance, the library automation project is understood as a definable process, but where in the flow of work does quality assurance take place? If it is at the end of the process and called "clean-up," then it is too late. One employee is paid to make a mistake while another employee is paid to correct the mistake. What good does it do to go online on schedule only to spend the following five years cleaning up a "dirty database"? The waste is obvious.

Point 4. End the Practice of Awarding Business on the Basis of Price Tag; Instead, Minimize Total Cost

Many libraries are part of state and local governments and governed by their purchasing rules, so it is very easy to stop reading at this point and say, "It won't work, my hands are tied." Deming recognized this limitation on government agencies.

> Without adequate measures of quality, business drifts to the lowest bidder, low quality and high cost being the inevitable result. American industry and the U.S. government, civil and military, are being rooked by the rules that award business to the lowest bidder.... The policy of forever trying to drive down the price of anything purchased, with no regard to quality and service, can drive good vendors and good service out of business. He that has a rule to give his business to the lowest bidder deserves to get rooked.

Rooked because the long-term benefits of quality (i.e., trust, durability, and trouble-free operation) have been traded for the short-term benefit of lower per unit price. The change proposed by Deming is—once again— revolutionary and is integrally related to an understanding, through education, of statistics and statistical process control.

In choosing CD-ROM services, for example, a reference librarian is faced with many options. Should price alone be a consideration? Never. It is reasonable for the librarian to send a questionnaire to companies asking such questions as: What is this company doing to insure a quality product? How does this company guard against typing mistakes? How does this company select software programmers? Is this company investing in long-term R&D of CD-ROM?

Deming points out: "The price tag is still easy to read, but an understanding of quality requires education."

Point 5. Improve Constantly and Forever the System of Production and Service

This concept ties together a variety of questions. How has the library's user changed since last year? How have I, professionally as a librarian, improved to meet this change? How have our vendors changed to meet this change? How has the cataloging process improved to meet this change? Improvements are changes, and improvement is constantly needed.

Point 6. Institute Training for All Employees

Librarians often mistake tours and orientation for training. Initial training actually teaches an employee how to do the required job within the culture of the organization. Understanding the new culture starts with an explanation of the library's mission statement. Corollary to this, the trainee must be taught where his or her particular job fits into the extended process or "big picture" of the organization.

Training is applicable to all levels of library employees. Reference librarians, for instance, should be trained in how other librarians conduct library instruction programs, reference interviews, and liaisons with subject selectors and not leave this solely to personal style. Personal style is essential to the concept of never-ending improvement, but can only be effectively used after the trainee understands the process.

Training, like any other process in the library, should be flow-charted and quality built in at each step in the training process. Statistical methods, which provide a baseline for accountability, should be employed to measure when the training is complete. Later, statistical feedback will also describe the worker's strengths so that they may complement other members of the team. Continually improving the training process should challenge top management in much the same way that parents are driven to give their children a better life than they had. This includes training librarians to be leaders.

Point 7. Adopt and Institute Leadership

Leaders understand the extended process, from the vendor all the way through to the user, and know how to statistically measure quality at each step in the process. Leaders nurture their staffs to become the very best at their jobs and that builds quality into the process. Leaders facilitate all ideas, even the lesser ones because they also know how to test new ideas before implementing change.

One method of testing the impact of new ideas was developed by Walter A. Shewhart, a statistician and a mentor of Deming. A typical application of the Shewhart Cycle (known as the Deming Cycle in Japan) occurred one semester when a library system was attempting to improve the turnaround time for ILL transactions among the eight libraries in the system. An example of how the Shewhart Cycle was used follows.

Step 1: What needs to be changed? The system of delivering ILLs via the weekly shuttle was too slow and expensive. But is it more or less expensive than sending materials through the mail? If it is more expensive, will the turnaround time be improved enough to justify the additional costs?

Step 2: Collect data, either previously available or through small-scale testing. A three-month test period was set up, during which time all ILL materials were mailed. Statistics on costs, including all personnel and materials costs, as well as turnaround time, were kept diligently.

Step 3: Observe the effects over time. After two months, one library dropped out of the experiment because it was too costly. The other libraries maintained the experiment through the three months. Notes and observations were kept by all participants.

Step 4: Study the results. The costs in postage were found to be higher than in using the shuttle (the shuttle would still run even without ILLs) but personnel and materials costs were the same. Turnaround time via mail, however, differed from weeks to days—a significant quality difference. ILL via mail was thus adopted.

Step 5: Using what was learned, repeat Step 1. One of the statistics discovered was that nearly all the libraries loaned more photocopies than monographs. How might switching to FAX affect the cost of the service?

Step 6: Repeat 2 and so on.

To have switched to using the postal service without testing the costs and impact would have been doing what Deming calls putting out fires or tampering. This type of planning and testing can be applied to any situation, large or small, and is a critical element in the culture of continuous improvement.

Point 8. Drive Out Fear

All fear is destructive, both to individuals and institutions. For an individual, fear on the job leads to withdrawal, high absenteeism, poor production, burnout, and even physical illness. For an organization, fearful employees mean that opportunities to improve production and quality are not being realized and that employee turnover is high.

In the Deming philosophy, driving out fear is an essential, paternal responsibility of management. Returning to the example used in the opening paragraph, what if Leslie, the second librarian, had been afraid to discuss the issue with the head of Public Services? What if she feared recrimination or being tagged a troublemaker? She would have been unhappy; service would have continued to be poor; Brooke, the first librarian, would not have been given the opportunity to learn and improve (but ultimately would have been held accountable); and the head of Public Services might just be counting up tally marks on the statistics sheet and thinking that everything is okay. Obviously, management—in this case, the head of Public Services— is responsible for seeing that the erring librarian is nurtured and retrained in a nonthreatening way that will instill not a fear of "being caught" the next time, but rather a sense of pride in seeking to deliver good service.

Point 9. Break Down Barriers Between Staff Areas

There are two kinds of barriers inherent to any organization: internal barriers and external barriers. External barriers are those that exist between the organization and its suppliers and clients. Internal barriers are those that exist between departments and service areas within the organization. In *The Deming Guide to Quality and Competitive Position* (Prentice-Hall, 1987), Howard and Shelly Gitlow identify several causes of organizational barriers:

competition, lack of communication, lack of constancy of purpose, lack of understanding of each service area's role in the total organization, personal grudges and jealousies, and differences in priorities are just a few.

The most destructive result of internal barriers is areas within the organization working at cross purposes with one another, creating hostility and competition. A classic example is the conflict between technical services and public services departments in libraries. Reference librarians in public services often complain that the subject headings are assigned by technical services librarians who are out of touch with what patrons need. Technical services librarians often complain that they are on a one-way street where they are expected to spend time on the reference desk but reference librarians don't have to spend time cataloging. When the time comes for everyone to sit down and work on the automation plan or revise the collection development policy, is it any wonder that little gets accomplished?

How are barriers eliminated? Each area must be committed to the organization's mission. Models and organizational charts are invaluable for establishing teams and networks at this point. Everyone in the organization must be willing to substitute teamwork for personal territory. In a total quality environment, employees understand the importance of all the service areas of the organization, have frequent meetings attended by everyone in the organization, and work together to analyze and study the processes of the organization.

Point 10. Eliminate Slogans, Exhortations, and Targets for the Work Force

"What is wrong with posters and exhortations?" asks Deming. "They are directed at the wrong people." "1990 is going to be a great year!!" boasted one library's posters and buttons welcoming students back. Although the budget had been cut severely again that year, and there was no support from the administration for adding extra hours on the reference desk or programs for user education, the reference librarian proudly wore her button, too. Posters and slogans are designed to create enthusiasm in individuals, but do nothing to improve faulty processes.

There is a danger in making the Deming philosophy itself a buzzword or slogan, particularly if the organization only pays lip service to the principles. An organization must adopt the philosophy of never-ending improvement and must take the necessary steps to improve the actual processes.

Point 11. Eliminate Numerical Quotas for the Work Force and Eliminate Numerical Goals for People in Management

It is easy to think that quotas are unique to manufacturing industries, but here are a just a few examples of numerical quotas common in libraries.

- Pages are required to be able to shelve 100 books per hour.

- Librarians are required to produce three bibliographies each year.

- Each temporary staff person hired to do retrospective conversion is required to process 50 books per hour.

At first it may seem that this point contradicts the emphasis placed on statistical control, but in reality it does not. In all these instances, these quotas emphasize short-term numerical goals over long-term quality.

In a total quality environment, the statement about shelving might be written as follows:

- Pages are responsible for correcting errors on their assigned shelves while they are shelving.

Statistics are used to measure the process by which ends are achieved, not the end results; it is a critical distinction. The theory is that if the process is under statistical control, a quality end product will follow naturally. How do we know, for instance, that materials are being shelved properly? Statistical sampling can plot the number of misshelved materials on a control chart that contains statistically established upper and lower limits. This will measure the quality of the shelving and may reveal variations that can then be addressed using procedures discussed earlier.

How many books should a page shelve in one hour? It doesn't matter. What matters is that the pages have been given the opportunity, through training, education, and an understanding of the process, to be successful in their jobs and to take pride in the good order of their assigned shelves.

Point 12. Remove Barriers That Rob People of Pride in Their Work

Provide employees with clearly defined job descriptions and the materials and support they need to do their jobs properly. Involve all members of the organization in the overall goals of the organization and entrust them with the responsibility for the quality of their own work. The traditional annual performance evaluation, popular in many libraries, creates fear, discourages cooperation, and encourages conformity to the point of shutting out creativity. It has no place in a Deming organization.

Point 13. Encourage Education and Self-Improvement for Everyone

A library adopting the Deming philosophy must first train the entire staff in the new principles of the philosophy and then in basic statistics (as in Point 6). Beyond this, training takes place at all levels, at all times. Without proper training and education, staff cannot be expected to do their jobs properly, which leads to low morale and fear. With continuing education, staff have reason to take pride in their work. Consider the difference between training and not training a reference librarian on new CD-ROM technologies, for example.

Retraining employees who are already established in their jobs is an essential element of the equation. No one is so expert that he/she does not need to develop new skills, keep abreast of technological changes, or be prepared for changes in the job. In the Deming world, retraining is a way of rewarding good employees, preparing employees for advancement, and preventing burnout.

Point 14. Take Action to Accomplish the Transformation

Quality does not come about by itself. It does not happen by telling people to work harder, by setting goals that encourage improvement, by threatening people with loss of their jobs, or by rewarding them with parking spaces. Quality results when every individual in the library understands and adopts the philosophy of never-ending improvement and when all the processes of library operations are in statistical control.

To this end, Deming is adamant that the pursuit of quality must begin from the top down; the program cannot be driven by middle managers or grassroots advocates. Top administrators must be willing to accept responsibility for initiating the transformation and implementing the 14 Points. With a long-term commitment and desire to change old habits, libraries can create a culture in which the quality of all the "products"—from answering the phone, to shelving books, to preparing programs, to planning new buildings, to answering reference questions—is continually improving.

TQM:
The Customer Focus

Susan Jurow

Director, Association of Research Libraries
Office of Management Services

There are two aspects of TQM that I believe could have a profound impact: the customer focus and the drive for constant improvement.

Recently, I had an opportunity to work with a mixed group of librarians, some from academic libraries and some from corporate libraries. A discussion ensued around the relationship between the library or librarians and their respective patron groups.

The special library professionals maintained they were more *client-centered* than academic librarians because they "had to be." They argued that they has to meet patrons' needs in order to justify the cost of their operations. The academic librarians hotly responded that they were just as *service-oriented*, providing an array of programs and services to a wide variety of patron groups.

As I listened, what I understood for the first time was the difference between being *client-centered* and being *service-oriented*. The former focuses on getting information about what the client wants and fulfilling those expectations. The latter means meeting what the librarian perceives as the patron's needs.

Librarians are caught in a dilemma because, as Michael Buckland points out, "...it is less clear why users sometimes do not seem to desire something they need.... This can be unsettling for librarians who are uniquely situated to know how the library service could be used to satisfy that need."[1]

A fundamental premise of TQM is that "You cannot focus solely on a product coming off the line or a person delivering a service and still be able to deliver quality to your customers."[2] Rather than trying to measure the quality of services and programs in the abstract, TQM links assessment of quality directly to the satisfaction of user needs.

Buckland also points out that staff and patron feedback about the quality of service are independent of each other and appear to have no effect on each other in the not-for-profit environment.[3] Academic and research libraries do not have the management information systems in

---

(From *ARL Current Issues*. Reprinted with permission of the Association of Research Libraries.)

place to gather, analyze, and understand patron behavior in a way that can improve the system as a whole.

In the past, evaluation processes have been used to regulate conformity to performance standards and measures. Resistance to scrutiny of one's efforts can often be attributed to a fear that the accomplishment will be found wanting.

TQM looks at assessment as a means of identifying areas for improvement. The purpose of understanding what is done and how it is done is to learn how to do it better. The gap between current level and desirable level is measured in order to close the gap, not to blame someone for the existence of the gap.

In discussing TQM, a senior library administrator said to me that is appeared to be old wine in new bottles. I agree that there is nothing new about meeting patron needs or measuring performance. However, I believe that TQM can provide us with both tools and a new attitude for thinking these issues.

References

1. Buckland, Michael. *Library Services in Theory and Context.* New York: Pergamon Press, 1983, p. 10.

2. Scholtes, Peter. *The Team Handbook.* Madison, WI: Joiner Associates, 1989, p. 2-6.

3. Buckland, p. 112.

Customer Focus—Obtaining Customer Input

Barbara Armstrong

National Quality Manager
National Information Resource Centre
Telecom Australia

Introduction

Total quality management (TQM) involves monitoring and assessing organizations and their products and services to identify opportunities for improvement, then taking action to make and maintain these improvements.

There are two main ways to determine those processes, activities, attitudes, or products which need to be monitored and improved:

a) input from staff, either informally or through formal staff surveys or staff suggestion schemes;

b) input from customers.

Staff input provides a good starting point because of their intimate knowledge of the factors that inhibit their ability to provide an excellent service. However, the ultimate judge of the quality of products and services is the customer.

The overall emphasis of TQM is on making the product or service match the requirements of the customers. Therefore, service providers must find ways to obtain information regarding customer needs, as well as their perception of the current level of performance. Given the limited resources available to information services, it is also important to determine the priorities for action—those issues that need improvement and that customers see as being important.

The following is a description of the three main (formal) methods used by Telecom Australia's National Information Resource Centre (NIRC) to obtain customer input and regularly review its products and services. The aims of these methods are to:

- ensure that products and services match the requirements of its customers and the business needs of the company.

(Original article printed with permission of the author.)

- determine the relative importance to the customer of various aspects of the products and services, and thereby setting priorities for action.

Two of the methods are used to examine the quality of a particular product or service. These are:

- regular **product surveys** of all customers of a particular value-added product, conducted at least annually, and more frequently if the topic or area covered by the product is particularly sensitive to change.

- ad-hoc **quality checks** of a particular service, such as a search or interlibrary loan, sent to customers who have just received that service.

The other method examines the **quality of the information service** as a whole from the viewpoint of the customer. This last method will be described first.

Method 1—Survey of Overall Service Quality

One of the tools of quality management, less well known than the famous "seven tools of TQM," is a planning method called quality function deployment (QFD). It aims to:

- identify customer requirements.

- determine priorities for action.

- translate customer requirements into the development or improvement of a product or service.

QFD is a planning method that helps organizations systematically focus on those features of a product or service that are most important to the customer. It helps an organization to be customer focused and customer driven. The areas in which QFD can be applied are wide ranging—from the global level of strategic planning to the more detailed level of determining the specific design elements for a particular product or service.

There are several approaches to QFD. Each of these approaches makes use of matrices to organize and relate pieces of data to each other—matrices that may be combined to form a house of quality.[1] The term "house of quality" has been used because the combination of the "rooms"—the axes and their relationships—result in a shape that looks like a house. The basic matrices and procedures can be adapted to the product, process, or project under consideration, to fit the particular needs.

As one of the main aims of QFD is the identification of priorities, it was decided to use a modified version of the QFD process to help identify customer requirements and priorities for action in the NIRC.

Mission and Scope

The starting point in QFD is to determine the mission and scope of the project, which for the NIRC was as follows:

1. To gain an understanding of our customers' perception of the quality of our services—their level of satisfaction with our performance;

2. To identify, in order of priority, those areas that need improvement, based on our customers' perception of how important each issue is to them.

As the NIRC is spread over six locations throughout Australia, points 1 and 2 were to be completed for each location, as well as for the NIRC as a whole.

The Customers

The next step is to decide who the customers of the product or service are—those whose opinions should be obtained. If desired, each customer group can be given a relative importance (weight). To ensure the essential needs of a particular group are met, the ratings from that group are emphasized relative to the ratings of other groups. For example, if your customers are employees of the company and you want to obtain and weight the requirements of the executive officers, middle management, and staff, you may give each group a rating such as the following:

Executives	0.5
Middle Management	0.3
Staff	0.2
Total	1.0

The customer weight must sum to "1" as above.

For the NIRC project no relative importance was given to each group, although as part of the study the importance and performance ratings of each group were compared.

Customer Requirements

The next requirement of QFD is a list of what the customer wants of the product, service, or issue under consideration, that is the voice of the customer, or the "whats." The items or criteria on this list are subsequently used in a survey which obtains information from customers about the importance of each item and their perception of the current level of performance.

QFD specialists advocate that the list of criteria be created from such methods as interviews, brainstorming sessions, or focus groups with customers. A number of the new management tools of TQM can help with this process—tools such as the Affinity Diagram or Tree Diagram. In reality, the most common way that a list of criteria is obtained is by interviewing employees, or by viewing the product or service from the customer's perspective.[2]

For the purpose of the NIRC project there already existed a list of key attributes of service quality that had been tested in a variety of service organizations. In 1988, Parasuraman et al. designed a survey instrument, called SERVQUAL, to compare customers' perceptions of the service they expected and the service they actually received, and thereby to measure the perceived quality of service.[3] Their survey instrument contained two parts—one form to measure the customers' expectations of all organizations of the type being investigated, and one to measure the perceptions of the particular organization being assessed. Their list of criteria was assessed to determine its usefulness for a survey of service quality in the field of information services.

During their work to establish a conceptual model of service quality Parasuraman et al. reported that "regardless of the type of service, consumers used basically similar criteria in evaluating service quality."[4] These seemed to fall into ten key categories:

Reliability

Responsiveness

Competence

Access

Courtesy

Communication

Credibility

Security

Understanding/knowing the customer

Tangibles

Subsequent testing led to these ten categories being condensed to five service quality dimensions, which Parasuraman et al. claimed could be used in any service.[5] The final five categories were:

Tangibles—physical facilities, equipment, appearance of contact personnel

Reliability—ability to perform the promised service dependably and accurately

Responsiveness—willingness to help customers and to provide a prompt service

Assurance—knowledge and courtesy of employees and their ability to inspire trust and confidence

Empathy—caring, individualized attention the company provides its customers.

Statements were included in the survey in order to identify the extent to which these service quality dimensions were being met.

One drawback of SERVQUAL's methodology is that it does not cope with the level of importance of each criterion. A customer may expect a service because of previous experiences, but that service may not be important to him or her in the business context. As Carmen reports: "[T]o most service providers, the importance of a particular service attribute seems more relevant than its expected level."[6] For the purposes of identifying problem areas and priorities for action, it is necessary to know what is important to the customers in their business operations. The identification of customers' perceptions of importance is a requirement of QFD.

Carmen found that the categories of service quality designed by Parasuraman et al. needed to be expanded or contracted according to the industry under review, as did the questions within the categories. He reports that "...when one of the dimensions of quality is particularly important to customers, they are likely to break that dimension into subdimensions" and "items will often need to be added for such dimensions."[7]

Therefore, while the SERVQUAL model was seen as a good starting point for a list of criteria for service quality within information services, and the design of a survey of service quality, modifications needed to be made.

Although the use of categories or dimensions is not a feature of QFD, it was decided to retain this aspect because of its usefulness in the analysis of results. Using SERVQUAL's list of five dimensions and related questions, service criteria were included, added, excluded, and the wording modified to suit the information services environment. The following changes were made to the original five dimensions:

- The majority of service encounters for the NIRC are via telephone or mail, because clients are located throughout Australia. Therefore, the whole service dimension of "tangibles" was excluded.

- In a competitive business environment confidentiality of information and information requests becomes a real issue. Therefore "assurance" became "assurance/security" to cover this aspect.

- As there were a large number of criteria relating to "communication," these were put into their own service quality dimension, with the definition: "keeping clients informed in a language they can understand, and listening to them."

- The criteria relating to "empathy" were included under "responsiveness."

Therefore the final four dimensions used by the NIRC were:

Reliability

Responsiveness/Empathy

Assurance/Security

Communication.

The dimension of "tangibles" would be included for organizations where this is relevant.

Survey Form Design

The Questions

Using this list of criteria, a survey form entitled "Survey of Service Quality" was designed and pilot tested. Four questions were asked:

1. When you have dealings with the NIRC, how important to you and your business operations is each of the following? (The criteria for service quality followed, listed in random sequence. That is, they were not grouped according to the four service quality dimensions [reliability, etc.] mentioned above. In fact, the quality dimensions were not included as headings or selections in the survey, but were used only for analysis of results.)

2. From your experience, what is the level of the NIRC's performance in each of the following areas? (The list followed, in a different sequence than that in Question 1.)

3. How would you rate the overall level of service you receive from the NIRC?

4. How willing would you be to recommend the NIRC to a colleague at Telecom?

Performance Scale

A five-point verbal rating scale was used on the survey form. These verbal ratings subsequently were translated into numeric scales.

A verbal scale helps customers translate their beliefs and perceptions to an identifiable rating level. It also helps with the interpretation of the end results, so that, for example, an average result of "4" has the meaning "good," not just the meaning "4."

Following pilot testing the final wording for the questions relating to performance, with the associated numerical scale was:

very poor	1
poor	2
fair	3
good	4
very good	5

A category for 'don't know' was also included.

Importance Scale

Originally the Importance Scale was designed along the same lines as the Performance Scale, with a midpoint and a range decreasing on one side and increasing on the other. However, because of the results of the pilot study the range was altered to a linear scale of increasing level of importance.

Customers believed that the issues listed were either unimportant or had an increasing level of importance; they did not relate to a scale that attempted to identify an increasing level of unimportance to one side of a midpoint.

It seems that customers think in two different ways for the two different issues—performance and importance. The use of the verbal scales helped to make this apparent and helped to ensure that the end results were not misinterpreted; the designer and the respondents were using the same meaning for the same rating level.

There were also difficulties with the relative strength of the wording of the Importance Scale. Originally the wording for the top level of the scale had been "very important," with the result that almost everything was very important and almost nothing was of average importance.

The final wording for the question relating to importance, with the associated numerical scale was:

unimportant	1
fairly important	2
important	3
very important	4
essential (crucial)	5

This resulted in a better spread of results across the range, allowing for better differentiation of priorities, which was the aim of the exercise.

Willingness Scale

The wording for willingness to recommend the NIRC to a colleague and the associated numerical scale was:

very unwilling	1
somewhat unwilling	2
neither willing nor unwilling	3
somewhat willing	4
very willing	5

It should be noted that the numerical ratings for importance and performance should not be directly compared, as the meaning and scale of each is different. While you may want something that has an importance rating of 5 (crucial) to have a performance rating of 5 (very good), the same cannot be said for the lower end of the scale—that something that has an importance rating of 2 (fairly important) should have a performance rating of 2 (poor).

The significance of the importance rating in the QFD process, apart from providing useful information about the relative importance of issues to customers, is its part as a weighting factor in the calculation of priorities—the issues that most need attention and improvement. For the purpose of assessing priorities, a simple comparison of the two numeric scales will provide misleading results.

On the survey form, columns were headed up with the appropriate word scale for the question being asked and were placed beside each list of criteria. Customers were asked to tick the column that best indicated their assessment of either the importance or current level of performance of each criterion.

Following the pilot test the wording of some of the criteria was altered to clarify the issue or use the customers' terminology. In addition, the key words of each question were underlined to help avoid confusion, particularly about the difference between questions 1 and 2.

Establish Importance and Performance

The results of the Survey of Service Quality were tabulated to gain the level of importance of each service quality issue, the level of performance in the same issues, the overall level of performance of the NIRC, and the customers' willingness to recommend the services of the NIRC. This was achieved by calculating the average of the responses to each criterion or question for each customer group surveyed and for the survey population as a whole.

The information obtained from the survey was also analyzed according to the service quality dimensions. This was achieved by calculating the average of all the responses to the criteria which were related to each service dimension.

It was found that to clients the most important service dimension is Reliability, while the dimension which had the greatest opportunity for improvement was Communication.

A useful, visual way to viewing and analyzing the comparative information is the X-Y grid. While the X-Y grid is not part of QFD, it is a simple tool, a visual system for comparing two values that are related in some way (see fig. 1). By using X-Y grids, the scope of opinion between groups or individuals can be displayed, or the positioning of issues, products or organizations can be demonstrated. In their book *Windows into Organisations*, John W. Newstrom and Jan L. Pierce report a variety of ways of using the grid to describe such things as management or leadership style, or strategies for competition and competitive advantage.

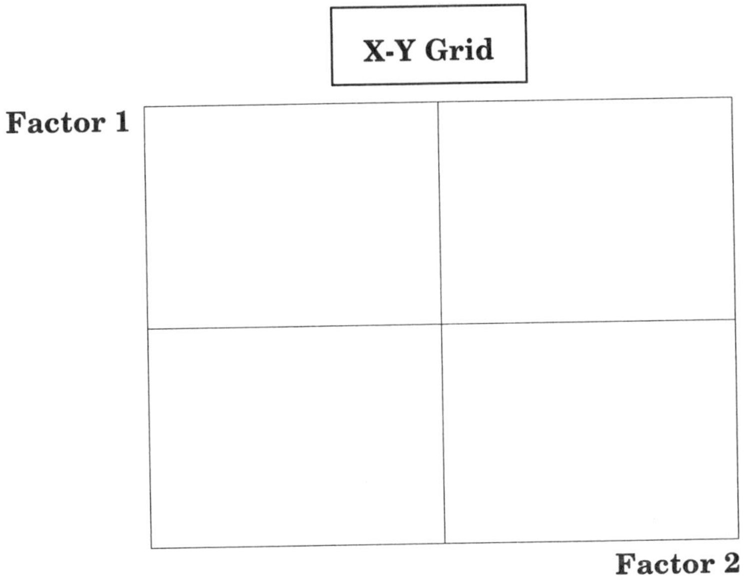

Fig. 1. X-Y Grid.

At the NIRC, X-Y grids were used to display the varied group opinions on the importance and performance of each criterion. The example shows how three groups (executive, managers, and other professionals) view the issue of confidentiality (see fig. 2).

An X-Y grid was also used to determine whether there was a good balance between the technical and people aspects of providing the information service.

In service industries every task has two aspects: a technical aspect (correct and competent use of procedures, rules, standards, equipment); and a people aspect (courtesy, caring, consideration, cooperation). A good balance of both technical and people skills is required to provide quality service. The X-Y grid can be used to compare these aspects of customer service and thus show where a service organization is positioned (see fig. 3 on page 29). In order to place the organization's current position on the service grid, the average of the performance responses for those criteria that fit under the category of "technical" should be calculated, then the same is done for the "people" category.

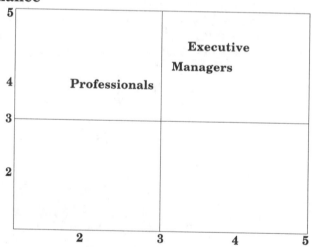

Fig. 2. Confidentiality.

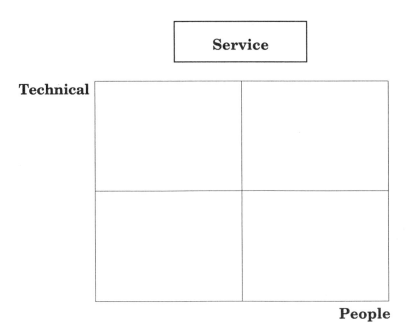

Fig. 3. Service.

The aim is to be positioned in the top right-hand box, showing that your organization gives excellent and equal attention to both the technical and the people aspects of providing an information service. Those organizations that are positioned in the top left-hand corner are good technically, but tend to be bureaucratic in their approach, following the rule book and giving little attention to the service contact or people aspects of service. Those in the bottom right-hand corner are lovely people to work with, but tend to ignore aspects such as timeliness and accuracy, or the need for technical excellence. And those in the bottom left-hand corner generally have a poor attitude to service provision, working for their own benefit and not for that of their customers.

Using the X-Y grid and the grouped results of a survey such as the Survey of Service Quality, a service organization can determine how clients perceive that organization in terms of the technical and people dimensions of client service. The grid can form one part of the measurement and analysis of service quality, and the establishment of priorities.

Establish Priorities for Action

As stated above, one of the main uses of QFD (and the reason why it was chosen for this NIRC project) is to assist organizations in determining their main priorities for action. Using the results of the survey, a formula is used to obtain a numerical score which gives each criterion a priority ranking.

Many factors may be used to establish priorities for action. These factors include:

- **the relative importance of each criterion or issue to customers—** the overall customer importance. If relative weightings have been given to each customer group, the average response for each group is multiplied by the assigned weight of that group and the results added together to form the overall customer importance.

- **the level of performance you are aiming to achieve** for each criterion, whether this be the ideal top score, the current performance level, or somewhere in-between (perhaps to match the level of your competitor).

- if desired, **additional "sales points"** for things that would be worth publicizing if marked improvements are made.

In the case of the NIRC's project

- as already stated, different weightings were not assigned to each customer group.

- it was decided that the level of performance to be aimed for should be made 5 (very good) for each criterion. The gap between the goal and the current performance level forms part of the "improvement ratio."

- additional points were included in the calculation of the level of priority of a criterion where there had been responses of "poor" or "very poor" for that particular criterion. These were the equivalent of sales points.

Each of the above factors was included in a formula to calculate a score that indicated the relative level of priority of each criterion.

$$\text{Priority} = \begin{array}{c} \text{Improvement} \\ \text{Ratio} \end{array} \times \begin{array}{c} \text{Sales} \\ \text{Points} \end{array} \times \begin{array}{c} \text{Overall Client} \\ \text{Importance} \end{array}$$

When the resulting scores were sorted into descending order, a ranked list of priorities for action was created.

Using the above formula issues that are highly important and have room for improvement rise to the top of the list, as do issues that are not as important but have performance responses of "poor" or "very poor". Issues that are not highly important and have a consistent performance of fair to very good remain towards the bottom of the list.

Priorities were determined for the NIRC as a whole and for each location. Regarding the latter, the relative importance given by local clients was used in the calculation, as well as the assessment of local performance, ensuring that the list of priorities for action reflected the perceptions and needs of the local clientele.

Method 2—Product Surveys

The NIRC produces a number of value-added products, each one designed for the key decision makers in a particular segment of the NIRC's customer base. These products are designed to be linked to the company's business aims and objectives, and surveys of each product are conducted at least once per year to ensure that each product remains relevant and focused on the needs of its customers and the business needs of the company.

The questionnaires are short (never more than one two-sided sheet) to encourage completion. Those who receive the product via e-mail are also sent the questionnaire via e-mail and are encouraged to return the results in like manner.

The questions asked are specific to each product, however the subject matter of the questions asked to date include:

- ratings for the product's presentation, layout and ease of reading, with a request for suggestions for improvement;

- a rating for the follow-up service if document delivery is required;

- ratings for the usefulness or importance of the topics/areas covered, with room for suggestions if there are perceived gaps;

- an indication of the ways in which the product is being used, and the ways in which the product has helped the reader;

- a rating for the overall value of the product to the reader;

- an indication of whether the product is circulated to others in the reader's work area.

Results from the last item have shown that the products are reaching a wide audience, thus reducing the unit cost of production, as well as indicating that the reader considers it sufficiently of value to be circulated to others.

Customers of the product are notified of the key results and actions arising out of the surveys. Individual queries are also followed up.

Method 3—Quality Checks

The design of these cards was one of several outcomes of the Survey of Service Quality described above. Customers believed that there was no quick and easy way for them to be able to provide feedback to the NIRC regarding their level of satisfaction with the service they had received. Using suggestions from customers and their input in pilot tests, two "quality check" cards were designed. One of the cards is used for services such as document delivery where the content and presentation of the product is not under the control of the NIRC; the other one is for services such as searches and the subsequent production of a report where the relevance and presentation of the product can be commented upon, as well as the timeliness of delivery.

The cards are designed to fit on one side of a card 10 cm. x 21 cm. (standard business envelope size) and contain very brief "tick the box" questions. They are sent out on an ad-hoc basis to check that the product which has just been sent, or the service which has just been received was as required. It allows for any problems to be notified and followed up immediately. It also checks if further information about the NIRC's products and services is required, enabling staff to focus their marketing presentations.

The cards can also be used by staff to record those informal verbal comments about the value of the service, or problems encountered, which might otherwise be lost and not acted upon.

Conclusion

All information services which aim to improve and maintain the quality of their products and services must find ways to obtain information regarding customer needs and their perceptions of the current level of performance. No one method will provide the complete picture. This paper describes three methods of obtaining the input to help determine the priorities for action—those issues that need improvement and that customers see as being important. Using these methods, it is not unusual to receive responses such as the following: "Good for you for conducting this survey" and "Well done for asking."

Notes

1. J. R. Hauser and D. Clausing. "The House of Quality," *Harvard Business Review*, May-June 1988, pp. 63-73.

2. Robert M. Adams and Mark D. Gavoor. "Quality Function Deployment: Its Promise and Reality," *ASQC Quality Congress Transactions*, San Francisco, 1990, pp. 33-38.

3. A. Parasuraman, V. A. Zeithaml, and L. L. Berry, "SERVQUAL: A Multi-Item Scale for Measuring Consumer Perceptions of Service Quality," *Journal of Retailing*, Vol. 64, Spring 1988, pp. 2-40.

4. A. Parasuraman, V. A. Zeithaml, and L. L. Berry, "A Conceptual Model of Service Quality and Its Implications for Future Research," *Journal of Marketing*, Vol. 49, Fall 1985, pp. 41-50.

5. Parasuraman et al., 1988.

6. James Carman, "Consumer Perceptions of Service Quality: An Assessment of the SERVQUAL Dimensions," *Journal of Retailing*, Vol. 66, Spring 1990, pp. 33-55.

7. Ibid., p. 50.

Quality Circles and Library Management

Daniel Sell
Mary Ellen Mortola

Daniel Sell is coordinator of the Staff & Instructional Development Department, Houston Community College System. His background includes experience as a library media specialist and instructional developer. Holder of an MLS degree, he will complete his doctorate in higher education administration this spring.

Mary Ellen Mortola is a public services librarian in the Houston Community College System. She supervises the industrial education branches of the library. She possesses an MLS and an MBA.

(This article is based on a presentation the authors made at the 1984 ALA Convention in Dallas.)

The use of Quality Circles is a management technique, a new approach to managing people and other resources in such a way as to achieve success in your library program.

Success (or excellence) has been making headlines the last few years. Last year alone, over thirty books and reports on excellence and quality in education and industry were published. Peters and Waterman's book, *In Search of Excellence*, made some important points about managerial excellence. In their analysis of companies which were achieving high levels of productivity, the authors noted that these companies were characterized by "unusual efforts on the part of apparently ordinary employees." These unusual efforts were present in companies that "gave their workers even a modicum of control over their destinies." The authors commented that administration in these companies foreswore organizational tidiness in favor of decentralization and autonomy in order to breed the entrepreneurial spirit and encourage innovation.

Psychologically, what else might contribute to our success as library managers? In *Relating Work to Education*, T. F. Green comments that understanding the distinction between work and a job is essential for understanding the problems of modern life. The central question, says Green, is always whether it is possible to find satisfaction in work through roles validated within the employment structure. What is often referred

(From *Community & Junior College Libraries* 3, no. 3. Copyright 1985. Reprinted with permission of Haworth Press, 10 Alice Street, Binghamton, NY 13904.)

to as alienation from work is seldom that. It is, rather, alienation from the job structure in a particular organization.

Larry Nelson, in his book, *Quality Circles and Japanese Style Management*, asserts a manager can assure his own success by recognizing and utilizing the talent of others. This requires the library manager to adopt a philosophy in day-to-day operations which includes the following points: (1) Management doesn't know all the problems; (2) Management is even less likely to know the solutions; (3) the employee is the expert and the closest to the problem; and (4) employees often have solutions if they are asked for them.

Definition of a Quality Circle

Quality Circles are small groups of people who do similar work and who voluntarily meet regularly to identify and analyze causes of problems, recommend solutions to management, and—when possible—implement those solutions.

Often bringing people together can be quite a chore. A quality circle brings together co-workers who have different jobs, backgrounds, prejudices, and personalities. Some may be enthusiastic about forming a group while others are either bored or disinterested. A few will be overly demanding. Still others will be skeptical or apathetic due to lack of knowledge about group interactions. But occasionally you may find a person who is extremely sociable and enjoys meeting with others. All of these types of people will have different ideas and expectations.

QCs meet voluntarily, usually on a weekly basis, to learn and then apply techniques for identifying, analyzing, and solving problems affecting their work or work place. The size of a circle can vary, but usually consists of seven or eight members who join voluntarily. No one is required to participate and no one is kept out. More than one circle may be operational within a department or library. Meetings, which generally last for one hour, permit members to:

1. Identify a theme or problem;

2. Receive technical training;

3. Analyze a problem;

4. Prepare recommendations for implementing a solution;

5. Present recommendations to management.[1]

The problems addressed are not restricted to those dealing with quality, but may be in any area that influences, directly or indirectly, the output of the work unit, such as safety, job structure, or the flow of information.

Among the members of the group is a facilitator who serves as the expert, the person experienced in the whole quality circle process. S/he is basically a support person, assisting the circle leader who is often a supervisor whom the facilitator has trained. The leader trains circle members in two techniques: problem solving and group processes. The circle works on one problem at a time and proposes solutions and action plans which are presented to management for approval.

History of the Quality Circle Movement

After World War II, when many industries in Japan had been destroyed, production was at a standstill; people were trying to survive the disaster. The quality of goods was known to be shabby; products seldom lasted for more than a day.

General Douglas MacArthur felt that something had to be done to improve the nation's image and asked the U.S. government to send someone to teach better quality control methods to the Japanese. Dr. Edward Deming, a statistician for the government, was sent to train management groups in Japan. During 1948 to 1950 he performed this job so successfully that he was called upon again and again to train more engineers and scientists in statistical methods. In 1951, the Japanese government honored his services by awarding the Deming Prize. Dr. Demings' philosophy, the Deming Wheel, stresses that everyone needs to plan, collect data, analyze, and construct his work to keep the circle rotating. This is how quality is properly maintained in a company.

During 1954-1955 another famous consultant, Dr. Juran, started visiting Japan. He lectured and preached what is know as "Total Quality Control" which begins in the design stage and ends after satisfactory services are provided to the customer.

The Japanese government then also became deeply involved in the service aspect of a quality improvement program. They began to broadcast radio and television programs on quality control, statistics, and related subjects. An entire month was proclaimed Quality Month and was marked by "Q" flags, quality slogans, seminars, and conventions. Slowly the Japanese image changed. Special checks and additional requirements were added for their exported products. By the 1970s the quality of Japanese products was no longer considered low. Today that quality in a number of fields—cameras, electronics, motorcycles, television sets, and radios—is considered to be number one. It took Japan thirty years of hardship and a constant striving for quality to become the third industrial power in the world.

Philosophy of Quality Circles

The basic philosophy behind QC is rooted in the human motivation theories of Maslow, Herzberg, and McGregor. In Maslow's concept of a hierarchy of needs, QC appeals to the highest-level requirements for self-esteem and self-fulfillment. Through involvement in the entire cycle from conceptualization to implementation of a problem-solving project, participants achieve significant goals enhancing their own sense of competency.

The quality circle concept fills Herzberg's admonition that motivation must be found in the work itself by incorporating learning, direct communication, feedback, responsibility, and recognition. Circle members participate enthusiastically over extended periods, even without special financial incentives, because they feel their work is more rewarding and their own contributions more meaningful.

McGregor's Theory Y managerial behavior recognizes the intellectual potential of the average employee. QCs tap this potential by stimulating the desire of employees for creative expression. While motivation is a personal matter, it must be stimulated and nurtured from the top of the organization. Quality Circles are vehicles by which library management can directly and positively improve employee morale.[2]

One can take from Quality Circles what fits, works, and contributes to positive results and discard the rest. The long-term benefit of a better trained, more skilled and more confident employee is the greatest payoff.

Characteristics of a Quality Circle

Successful Quality Circles are characterized by:

1. Supportive management;

2. Team effort;

3. Emphasis on selecting objectives and identifying, investigating, and solving problems;

4. Focus on results;

5. Volunteer membership;

6. Provision of training for both workers and management;

7. Open and positive attitudes.

Quality Circles Objectives

The success of Quality Circles as a management tool depends upon setting goals and objectives, including the following:

1. Self-development—to train individuals in the company's needs and sharpen their abilities;

2. Mutual development—to work toward group cooperation and mutual understanding;

3. Quality—to achieve a quality image and the quality of the product or service;

4. Communication—to develop positive attitudes through improved communication in frequently-held group meetings;

5. Waste reduction—to cut down waste in material, rework, and time;

6. Job satisfaction—to help satisfy the "achievement needs" of employees by giving serious consideration to their ideas;

7. Cost reduction—a value analysis—to reduce cost without reducing quality;

8. Productivity—to improve productivity by reducing costs and eliminating rejects and dissatisfied customers;

9. Safety—to constantly monitor safety problems and install safety measures which improve the working environment;

10. Problem solving—to offer employees a chance to come together, think about problems, hash them out, and pool ideas to formulate solutions;

11. Team building—to create team spirit and mutual cooperation;

12. Problem prevention—to anticipate problems before they occur;

13. Involvement—to improve productivity by creating in employees a greater interest in their jobs;

14. Participation—to create cohesiveness and unity in the institution;

15. Reduction of absenteeism—to reduce lost time and grievances.

Relationship with Library Management

In a recent issue of *Special Libraries*, Mourney and Mansfield quote Donald Dewar to illustrate the focus of Quality Circles:

> Think of quality circles, not as a cure-all, but as a unique tool with which to generate an atmosphere in which people can solve their problems: changing from reactive putting out fires to proactive anticipation and seeking improvements.[3]

Quality Circles have been successful in industry where work output and profits can be measured. But generally speaking, libraries do not operate at a profit nor can their success always be quantitatively defined. However, quality is a concern and can be extended to quality of service, information required, individual performance, and many other areas.

The Japanese view quality as a concept beyond conformance to a standard of workmanship. Quality for them means user satisfaction or the product's fitness for use. This is an important notion in considering the improvement of information delivery services and setting both short- and long-term library goals.

Consider the example of a lowly, full-time evening reference librarian who walked into work early one afternoon to discover her desk on the opposite end of the library and her filing cabinet quite a distance from her work area—her home completely rearranged during the morning by the library director. Did the director know why the furniture was previously in a certain arrangement? That it allowed the librarian to view the circulation desk during the evening when the clerk went on a break or was running around campus picking up audio-visual equipment? And didn't this same library director also try to remove the phone from the library circulation desk because it was the line least used? She was unaware that in the evening when the reference librarian was in the stacks helping patrons, that phone was the easiest to reach? It was the only phone that could be pulled onto the counter in view and earshot of all the evening staff.

These changes were not only unproductive, but they caused unnecessary resentment and ill-will among the staff. Mistrust arose between the day and evening staff and even the faculty began to take sides as the rift grew. People who could have been working together to achieve a harmonious atmosphere were instead working in opposition, creating chaos and losing sight of the services they were supposed to be providing.

Consider quality potential with your own library:

1. Within the library staff: Public Services vs. Technical Service.

2. Between library and faculty: Faculty advisory committees—are they quality circles?

3. Between library and outside borrowers: Service at the circulation desk. Quality of product.

Houston Community College System has the largest film library in Houston. Over 120 companies borrow films from our library. Recently, however, we had the experience of being on the receiving end. We participated in a forum presented by the local chapter of the American Society of Training and Development (ASTD). Our library, together with the sales and marketing division of the college, shared an exhibit booth at this event. We had borrowed ten films from the library to show at this booth to attract interest both in the college and in the library. To our chagrin, three of the films were unusable: one had damaged sprocket holes, another had insufficient leaders, so that the beginning and end of the film were cut off, and the third film was not the one indicated on the outside of the can. We concluded that if our reliability was only 70 percent, we needed to do something about our service.

One way to go about solving these reliability problems would be to create a quality circle consisting of the media booking clerks, the circulation supervisor, the subject specialist, and the marketing representative for the film library.

Creating a Quality Circle

A steering committee, consisting of library department heads or representatives should be established to set the goals, objectives, and operational guidelines for Quality Circles. A facilitator—or facilitators, if you have a very large library staff—should be recruited (and not drafted) from your staff. This person acts as the in-house expert and consultant and trouble shooter for all the quality circles. The facilitator should report directly to the Library Director, if possible. In addition, the facilitator reports quality circle progress and problems to the steering committee. Great care should be exercised in selecting a facilitator. This person must have human and interpersonal relations skills and should be able to conduct training sessions and generally assist circles in overcoming obstacles.

The circle itself should consist of six to ten people with similar job functions, such as circulation, media services, cataloging, etc. Most of the literature recommends that the leader in each circle be that group's supervisor, at least initially. This will help insure management's active commitment to and participation in the projects. Supervisors should not feel their authority is being undermined. During the circle meeting, the circle leader is considered a part of the group. Quality Circles should not impose another organizational hierarchy on your existing library management structure. The QC model should blend into your existing hierarchy. For example, does the director already meet regularly with department heads? Quality Circle steering committee functions could become a formalized portion of that meeting's agenda.

Careful planning is essential before setting up meetings. During the planning stages you will need to train circle leaders in many of the techniques described later in this article and generally create an atmosphere conducive to quality circle success. Dr. Juran, in his article, "Development of Quality Circles in Japan," reminds us that a quality circle is only *one* element in achieving success. Other essentials he cites include a *long-term* commitment to human resources development and improvements in quality, a strong commitment to positive reinforcement, and a considerable expenditure of time and money for training/meetings which are not just adjunct activities to the "actual work" being carried on.

Implementing Quality Circles

Each quality circle decides what it will work on. The group should be concerned only with those work-related problems experienced by its members: in other words, problems within their expertise. Some of the day-to-day problems a group might want to address could deal with shelving, reference assistance evaluation, book acquisition procedures, circulation desk routines—in short, anything that could use improvement.

Training should be on-going. Quality Circles should be given some initial training, then put to work. As they encounter difficulties, they will then be receptive to a second training session designed to help them with their actual problems.

The Quality Circle implements solutions. This is the point at which some administrators drop the ball. The purpose of quality circles is not only to identify problems, but to solve them. This requires an open door and an open mind in the Library Director's office. Even more important, credit for a solution *must* go to the group that developed it. This concept of "ownership" is important because it boosts morale.

Quality Circles must have access to resources and information. QC leaders must be able to clear stumbling blocks and communicate openly within and between groups. The way one group addresses its problems may impinge on the work of another group. It may also require information from other groups or departments. Nothing could be worse than to have a quality circle arrive at a solution, only to find the entire process had been pre-empted by a management decision or plan unknown to them.

Management should be supportive. Management can enhance the status of a quality circle by valuing its presentations and by observing, on occasion, its meetings. Library management should communicate to others throughout the college the positive results gained from the time invested in quality circles.

Quality Circle Techniques

Many of the techniques used in Quality Circles are familiar to most library managers. Using any of them will depend on the level of sophistication of the group. Some of the more commonly used techniques are:

- Problem Identification through Brainstorming or Nominal Group Technique

- Data Collection and Display

- Data Analysis—Force Field or Cause and Effect

- Group Dynamics

- Leadership

- Communication

Many of these skills are important tools which library personnel can utilize in a number of other settings, such as in serving on college-wide committees. Therefore, you will be providing your staff with opportunities and skills for personal professional growth.

Measuring Progress: Benefits

Quality circles can improve productivity, provide better solutions to problems, improve the quality of working life, and augment staff decision-making skills. Other benefits include: (1) quality, product, attitude, communication, and productivity improvements; (2) staff participation; (3) cost and waste reductions; (4) machine utilization and maintenance; (5) safety enhancements; (6) patron satisfaction; and (7) work satisfaction which reduces absenteeism and grievances. Quality circles can generate real changes in people when they are permitted to utilize their creativity and problem-solving skills to the fullest.

Quality Circle Limitations

Quality Circles is a management tool which is deceptively simple. That is why management support and organizational readiness are so important. We would not recommend, for instance, mandating QCs across the board in libraries accustomed to an autocratic management style. Libraries must be prepared to schedule personnel to attend weekly meetings. Both work groups and management might have unreasonable expectations. Both might become impatient or be resistant to change or feel they're being manipulated.

Quality Circles will not solve all library problems. Libraries do not operate in a vacuum; many decisions, events, and policies outside their control can have a tremendous impact on QC programs. And there are occasions when quick decisions are necessary. Don't promise too much when starting up a program and proceed slowly.

The facilitator must be carefully chosen and must be a competent, "people person." S/he must be able to keep the group "on track." Moreover, this person must have the respect of group members and the trust of top management. Attrition is also a problem, not only in the case of facilitators, but also in regard to group members and library managers. In fact, the literature recommends you do *not* implement quality circles if you anticipate any major changes in the library organization in the near future.

QCs incorporate a participative management style. Many tend to think of any loose discussion group as a quality circle, not realizing the necessary long-term commitment to training, group interaction, rigorous *step-by-step* improvements, and plain, old-fashioned hard work involved. Group consensus, a quality-circle imperative, is much more difficult to achieve than group majority rule. A QC program implies that your library has decided to prize teamwork more than competition.

Conclusion

Columbia University's Institute of Higher Education polled a nationwide sample of faculty in 1970 and again in 1980. The study found that the "decline in faculty morale is unrelated to changes in college income or average faculty salary." Rather, the study determined, "it is the faculty member's involvement in planning and in the governance of their institutions that has the greatest effect on their morale, on their commitment to the purposes of the college, and on their support of its administration."[6] Hopefully, library managers will heed the results of this study, and will consider tailoring the Quality Circle concept to their unique situation and needs.

Reference Notes

1. Charles Matrell & John Tyson, "QWL Strategies: Quality Circles," *The Journal of Academic Librarianship* (November 1983): 285-87.

2. "Quality Circles," *1984 McGraw-Hill Yearbook of Science and Technology*, pp. 32-37.

3. "Quality Circles for Management Decisions." *Special Libraries* (April 1984): 87-94.

4. Dr. Zane K. Quible, "Quality Circles: A Well-Rounded Approach to Employee Involvement," *Management World* (September 1981): 10-11, 38.

5. Sud Ingle, *Quality Circle Master Guide* (Englewood Cliffs, NJ: Prentice-Hall, 1982).

6. Jack Magarrell, "Decline in Faculty Morale Laid to Governance Role, Not Salary," *The Chronicle of Higher Education* (10 November 1982): 1-28.

References

Ackley, P. "Quality Circles in Education: Getting Down to the Nitty Gritty," *Thrust* (November/December 1982): 12-14.

Alexanderson, B. Orjan. "QC Circles in Scandinavia," *Quality Progress* (11 July 1980): 18-19.

Ambler, Aldonna & Overholt, Miles. "Are Quality Circles Right For Your Company?" *Personnel Journal* (November 1982): 829-831.

Blake, Robert R. & Mouton, Jane Srygley. *Productivity: The Human Side.* New York: AMACOM, 1981.

Bonner, J. S. "Japanese Quality Circles: Can They Work in Education?" *Phi Delta Kappan* (June 1982): 681.

Bruce-Briggs, B. "The Dangerous Folly Called Theory Z." *Fortune* (17 May 1982): 41-53.

Dailey, John J. & Kagerer, Rudolph L. "A Primer on Quality Circles." Supervisory Management (June 1982): 40-43.

Day, Charles R., Jr. & Pascarella, Perry. "Righting the Productivity Balance." *Industry Week* (29 September 1980): 50-59.

Dewar, Donald. *Quality Circle Guide to Participation Management.* Englewood Cliffs, NJ: Prentice-Hall, 1980.

____. "Quality Circles." *1984 McGraw-Hill Yearbook of Science & Technology.* New York: McGraw-Hill, pp. 33-37.

Drucker, Peter. *Management Tasks, Responsibilities, Practices.* New York: Harper and Row, 1973.

Gillett, Darwin. "Better Quality Circles: A Need for More Manager Action." *Management Review* (January, 1983): 19-25.

Green, T. F. "Ironies and Paradoxes," in *Relating Work and Education,* Dychman W. Vermiley (ed.) San Francisco, CA: Jossey Bass, 1977, pp. 42-44.

Gyma, Frank M., Jr. *Quality Circles: A Team Approach to Problem Solving.* New York: American Management Association, 1981.

Hanley, Joseph. "Our Experience With Quality Circles," *Quality Progress* (February 1980): 22-26.

Holt, Larry C. & Wagner, Thomas E. "Quality Circles: An Alternative For Higher Education." *Journal of the College and University Personnel Association* (Spring 1983): 11-14.

If Japan Can ... Why Can't We? (Videorecording) Wilmette, IL: Films, Inc., 1980.

Ingle, Sud. *Quality Circles Master Guide.* New York: Prentice-Hall, 1982.

Jenkins, Kenneth M. & Shimada, Justin. "Quality Circles in the Service Sector." *Supervisory Management* (August 1981): 2-7.

Jones, W. G. "Quality's Vicious Circles." Management Today (March 1983): 97-98.

Juran, J. M. "International Significance of the QC Circle Movement." *Quality Progress* (November 1980): 18-22.

Juran, J. M. "Development of Quality Circles in Japan." *Statistical Quality Control 26* (March 1975): 18-24.

MacAdam, M. "Multidimensional Quality Circles: Tool to Renew the Educational Enterprise." *Thrust* (January 1984): 10-12.

Martell, Charles & Tyson, John. "QWL Strategies: Quality Circles." *The Journal of Academic Librarianship* (November 1983): 285-287.

Metz, Edmund, Jr. "Caution: Quality Circles Ahead." *Training and Development Journal* (August 1981): 71-76.

Mourney, Deborah A. & Mansfield, Jerry W. "Quality Circles for Management Decisions: What's in it for Libraries?" *Special Libraries* (April 1984): 87-94.

Nelson, Larry L. *Quality Circles and Japanese Style Management*. Milwaukee, WI: Measurable Performance Systems, Inc., 1982.

Pascarella, Perry. "Quality Circles: Just Another Management Headache?" *Industry Week* (June 1982): 50-55.

People and Productivity: We Learn from the Japanese. Motion Picture. Chicago: Encyclopaedia Britannica Educational Corp, 1982.

Peters, Thomas J. *In Search of Excellence*. New York: Warner, 1982.

"Quality Control Circles: They Work and Don't Work." *Wall Street Journal* (29 March 1982): 18.

Quible, Dr. Zane K. "Quality Circles: A Well-Rounded Approach to Employee Involvement." *Management World* (September 1981): 10-11, 38.

Romaine, Larry. "Quality Circles That Enhance Productivity." *Community and Junior College Journal* (November 1981): 30-31.

Sacharow, Fredda. "Companies Are Running in Circles and Success Stories Are Running In." *Philadelphia Inquirer* (December 1982): 10-J.

Unger, Harlow G. "New Americans Swarm Japanese Plants to Learn QC and Productivity." *New England Purchaser & Connecticut Purchaser* (May, 1980): 23-25.

"Will the Slide Kill Quality Circles?" *Business Week* (11 January 1982): 108-109.

Quality Circles: Realistic Alternatives for Libraries

Nancy Hanks, Director
B. D. Owens Library

Dr. Stan Wade, Professor
College of Education
Northwest Missouri State University, Maryville

The concept of "quality control" is an accepted cornerstone of American business. Consumers today expect quality, and products or services which do not offer the assurance of quality are not given high regard. As public-supported, service-based organizations, libraries must provide quality collections and services to their clienteles or lose their support.

Typically, the library administrator assumes total responsibility for the library's operations. If the administrator wants or requires input, he or she forms a committee, but usually no systematic process is employed to solve the library's problems or to help in major decision making. There are many ways to involve librarians and the library staff in organizational matters, but one relatively new approach is the use of quality circles.

The quality circle, a technique developed by Japanese industrialists to improve company productivity, is a small group of employees that shares related work experience and volunteers to meet on a regular basis to identify, analyze and solve problems.

While it would be ideal for members of a library quality circle to work in one area, such as technical services, they should at least be familiar with a job or interact closely enough so that each problem will be important to all of them. There is no limit to the number of quality circles which could be created in a library setting. However, small libraries might have only one group due to the overlapping of responsibilities and sharing of duties.

Skeptics of quality circles have indicated that they could not work outside of the corporate setting, but they have been used effectively by public agencies. The quality circle does not offer a quick solution to a problem, but does provide a thorough examination of it by the individuals most closely related to the situation under examination. Quality circles have been credited with achieving high quality and improved productivity while increasing employee morale in the business sector. Because the members of a circle can

(Reprinted with permission from *Show Me Libraries*, Missouri State Library.)

44

be problem solvers as well as workers, they feel more involved, more a part of the organization. With an improvement in staff satisfaction as a result of their additional involvement, there may also be an improvement in the quality of service to the public—a realistic goal for a library.

There are some aspects of quality circles which make its use difficult for those organizations without numbers of people who share the same job. Only very large libraries, for example, have five catalogers or five circulation librarians to form a quality circle, and it is critical for the individuals in the circle to do the same or closely related work. But it is possible to adapt the steps in the quality circle concept to improve the quality of library service.

Prior to implementing quality circles, it is imperative that a clear understanding be formulated that points out precisely what the function of the circles will be. The primary concern of a circle should relate to the immediate work group and not the organization as a whole. Therefore, issues such as salary, promotion, vacations, grievances, etc. would not be appropriate for circle consideration. On occasion, a circle may choose a problem which exists outside the immediate work area. When this occurs, representatives from other areas affected should be involved in working with circle members in achieving a solution to the problem. For example, a circle composed of circulation personnel may choose to work on the problem of damage and destruction of materials. In this case, it may be necessary to involve some staff members from the areas of reference and cataloging.

Many organizations assume that anytime they permit their people to get together and discuss common problems they are utilizing the quality circle concept. Although this may be a beginning, it is where quality circles make a radical departure from the commonly-held social gathering or gripe sessions conducted under the euphemism of participative management. In order to maximize the effectiveness of quality circles, it is essential that all participating members receive the necessary training in group problem-solving methods and procedures. This can be accomplished in about 24 hours by self-training or by an outside consultant. Two outstanding sources for member training are *How to Make Meetings Work* by Michael Doyle and David Straus[1] and *The Quality Circles Handbook* by Donald Dewar.[2]

The following steps are considered by the writers to be appropriate for use by libraries in utilizing quality circles.

1. *Identify Problems*

The first true test of a manager's, in this case the library director's, commitment to quality circles surfaces during the initial problem identification stage. If library employees are expected to work only on boss-imposed problems, the circle is merely a reflection of what library management considers important. It is an extremely important concept of quality circles that circle members themselves identify the problems that they deem important to their particular work area. This does not preclude management from submitting problems to be considered to the circles. However, in order for circles to function effectively, they must have freedom to identify those problems in their work area which they think are important and will enhance their quality of performance.

During the problem identification phase, it is desirable that all members participate freely in the process. Brainstorming, if used properly, is an effective means of producing a large number of creative ideas and encourages the participation of all members of the circle. During this phase, all problems should be listed without evaluation from group members. It is highly recommended that large sheets of butcher paper and a person to act as a recorder be utilized to record and keep for future use all relevant information exchanged during circle meetings.

2. *Problem Selection*

After the list of problems has been generated, circle members should select a problem that they can agree to work on. This is an important step in arriving at a successful solution. It is advisable that circles work on only one problem at a time and that other problems identified by the group be saved for future consideration.

New circles should limit their initial problem selection to their immediate work area and select one of the less-complex problems that can be solved in a relatively short period of time.

3. *Problem Definition*

Once a problem has been identified by the group, the natural tendency is to jump in and start working on solutions. Consequently, much time may be wasted on problem symptoms or member misconceptions rather than on the real problem. For example, a person might suddenly start performing poorly at work. The individual appears unmotivated and unconcerned about his/her work. Treating these symptoms would be to no avail if the real problem turns out to be friction with supervisor over unfair evaluation. Therefore, time spent on gaining a clear understanding of the problem by all members of a group will pay dividends later when solutions to the problem are being considered.

Prior to defining the problem, it is often helpful to record members' perceptions of the problem. It is possible that several members of the group will initially have totally different views on what the real problem is. Divergent views should be encouraged and not evaluated at this time. Once each individual has had an opportunity to give his/her perception of the problem, it is appropriate to identify specific facts which will bring the "real" problem into focus. A successful technique for gathering facts is to determine what "is" and what "is not" a consequence of the problem.

Facts associated with the five "W's" and "H" will assist in defining the problem.

a. *Who?* Who in the library is/is not involved and affected? Who has the necessary knowledge or expertise about the problem?

b. *What?* What is/is not true about the problem? What are the actual signs of the problem? What effect does the problem have?

c. *When?* When does the problem occur/not occur?

d. *Where?* Where does the problem occur/not occur?

e. *Why?* Why does problem occur/not occur?

f. *How?* How frequently does the problem occur? How much does the problem affect our organization?

Facts gained by the above exercise will assist members in writing a problem statement. The problem statement should be phrased in broad and open-ended terms. For example, a problem statement concerning overdue books which reads "Should fines for overdue books be increased?" does not offer other alternatives for solving the problem of overdue books. Also, the statement represents a solution to the problem rather than a problem statement. It is more appropriate to state the definition in broader terms beginning with a "how to," open-ended question. The problem with overdue books might be stated as, "How do we reduce the number of overdue books?"

4. *Problem Analysis*
In order to arrive at a quality solution to a problem, it is crucial that the solution be based upon accurate and reliable information rather than opinions or guesses. During the analysis phase, accurate information is gathered that has a significant bearing on the problem.

The first step is to determine what types of information are needed in order to understand the problem fully. The basic questions of who, what, where, when, why, and how are helpful in determining what information is required. Once the nature of the information has been decided, it is then necessary to determine how the information will be collected. Some of the more common methods of collecting data are interviewing, observation, documentation, questionnaires and sampling. Any one or a combination of these procedures may be appropriate depending upon the type of information desired.

Two other methods which may be used to analyze a problem when circle members already possess the necessary information are cause and effect analysis and force-field analysis.

Cause and Effect Analysis—Starting the problem in a box to the right and then using a fishbone diagram (see illustration below), members brainstorm possible causes of the problem. Possible causes are usually grouped into one of four categories: methods, machines, materials and people power.

Fishbone Analysis

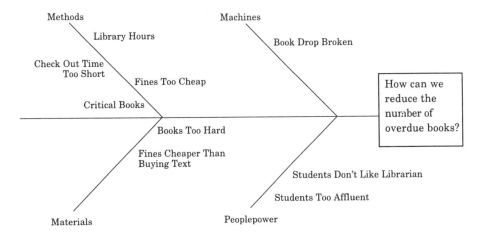

During the brainstorming session, circle members should be cautioned to list causes of the problem and not solutions. After all of the possible causes have been listed, the members vote on the most likely causes that produce the effect (problem). The major cause or causes will then need to be verified by another brainstorming session or the collection of additional data.

Force-Field Analysis—Another way to analyze a problem is to list those forces that are sustaining the problem from getting worse and those forces which are restraining it or keeping it from getting better (see illustration below). Once analyzed, the objective during the problem solution phase is to generate alternatives that will increase the sustaining forces while reducing the restraining forces.

Force Field Analysis

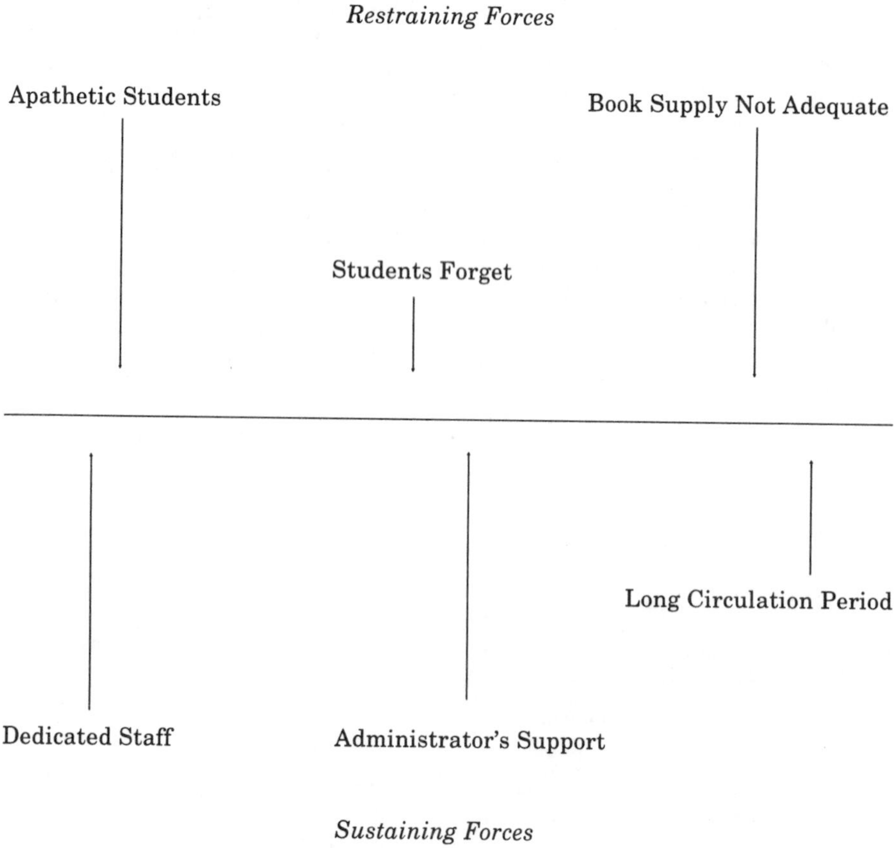

Restraining Forces

Apathetic Students

Book Supply Not Adequate

Students Forget

Long Circulation Period

Dedicated Staff

Administrator's Support

Sustaining Forces

5. *Generating Alternatives*

After the cause or causes have been verified, it is time to start working on alternatives to solve the problem. This can best be done by employing a creative brainstorming session where all ideas are accepted without evaluation. The more ideas generated at this time the greater the potential will be for finding a viable solution to the problem.

6. *Solution Selection*

In order to achieve a win/win attitude during this phase, it is essential that circle members have common agreement on what they want for an outcome. In other words, what criteria will be used to determine what alternative or alternatives will provide the best solution or solutions to the problem. Once the criteria have been agreed upon, the alternatives are evaluated accordingly. If more than one alternative meets the desired criteria, then it is desirable to look at the advantages and disadvantages of each alternative.

Every possible effort should be made during this phase to achieve group consensus on selecting the solution to the problem. This may be enhanced by selecting more than one solution alternative, or by combining or eliminating parts of two or more alternatives.

7. *Management Presentation*

If implementation of the solution is dependent upon approval outside the purview of the quality circle, then the solution must be recommended to higher management, probably the library director. The management presentation provides circle members the opportunity for recognition and all members should participate. Charts and graphs made from each step in the problem-solving process will assist in the management presentation. Since the type of charts and graphs will be dependent upon the method and format used during data collection, the authors suggest you refer to Donald Dewar's *The Quality Circles Handbook*. Studies reveal that an excess of 80 percent of the recommendations by quality circles are approved by management.

Steps to Establish a Quality Circle in a Library

1. Examine the leadership style of the library's administration to determine if quality circles could be used comfortably. Less than a total commitment from the library director will result in a less than successful attempt to establish a quality circle.

2. Become familiar with quality circles by reading books and articles about them and their use.

3. Train someone on the library staff to be a facilitator.

4. Involve the staff in the planning of quality circles.

5. Ask for volunteers to form the quality circle.

6. Provide training for the members of the circle.

7. Establish a meeting time and place.

References

1. Doyle, Michael, and David Straus. *How to Make Meetings Work*. Chicago: Paperboy Press, 1979.

2. Dewar, Donald. *The Quality Circles Handbook*. Red Bluff, California: Quality Circles Institute, 1980.

Why Not Consider Quality Circles?

Gina Speakman

*Gina Speakman is an Information Officer with Knowsley Careers
Service, Liverpool, UK.*

What Are Quality Circles?

"A quality circle (QC) is a group of 4-12 people from the same work
area who meet voluntarily and regularly to identify, investigate, analyse
and solve their own work-related problems. The circle presents solutions
to management and is involved in implementing and later monitoring
them." This is the definition from the National Society of Quality Circles,
which was founded in 1982 for the promotion and education of quality circles.
It is estimated that over 500 organisations use them and the number is
growing fast. Firms such as Kodak, Wedgwood, Marks & Spencer, Ford,
Blackwells, health authorities and water companies all use them.

The circle usually meets once a week, with a trained supervisor, in
work time for half to one hour to discuss niggling local issues and suggest
ways of solving these problems. The supervisor has the role of setting up
the group and then acting as its leader. The supervisor will guide and
draw together the group so that its members are able to tackle and solve
quality problems. Ideally the group should meet in a quiet room away from
the main work area.

So, having established what a quality circle is, what are the objectives
of this circle?

(1) To put its own house in order.

(2) To be responsible for selecting the problems it wishes to tackle in
order to achieve.[1]

(3) To involve staff in decision making within the organisation.

(4) To develop people in the organisation through the acquisition of
new skills and the opportunity to work together on "real-world"
problems. Supervisors can also develop their skills in problem
solving and in leading small groups.

(5) To generate benefits for the organisation and the people in this organisation. It is important that this is seen as being not only cost-effective but also "people"-effective.

The criteria necessary to achieve these objectives are:

(1) All members must be voluntary, including the supervisor—this freedom generally ensures a high level of commitment to attend and participate. This has a knock-on effect of creating a sense of owner-ship and responsibility for the job as well as fostering team spirit.

(2) All management must be committed to the concept. This is vital, if quality circles are to have the chance to work, because a background supportive management role will be seen as encouragement. A good QC will feel able to invite management in to clarify a particular point. Of course management should take any final decision, but QCs should be able to have authority to speed up solutions. When the QC does not have authority, it should make a presentation to the managers, proposing any solutions. However, it is imperative for the continued good working of the QC that management should explain fully their reasons if a proposal is not accepted.

(3) There must be good training and introduction to their usage. Also it has been found through experience both in America and the UK that it is vital that a facilitator is appointed and trained first to co-ordinate the programme and that he/she is prepared to set aside an agreed time to make QCs work. This will probably involve sitting in on the first few circles and assisting in the training of the supervisor and the group.

This training should cover the following:

(1) How to use brainstorming to identify a problem.

(2) Methods of data collection.

(3) Presentation skills.

(4) Meeting skills.

It is to be hoped that, if training is structured properly and carefully, QCs will use skills acquired to concentrate on solving problems and action planning. They should not become a grumbling session or discuss non-relevant subjects but should collect data objectively to suggest ways of improving quality or reducing costs. Quality circles are about practicalities, not theories, and their aim is to produce positive results and conclusions.

Plan of Action

(1) Members list any problems of which they know.

(2) Team establishes priorities.

(3) Team discusses solutions (sometimes one problem may be dis-cussed by a sub-group if they are particularly knowledgeable in that area); they then report back to the main group.

It might be useful to use a six-point checklist at meetings:

(1) Can we solve this problem?

(2) How long will it take to solve it?

(3) Will it assist our QC training?

(4) Can we collect data about this particular problem?

(5) Is the solution viable and cost-effective?

(6) Last but not least—do we really want to do it?

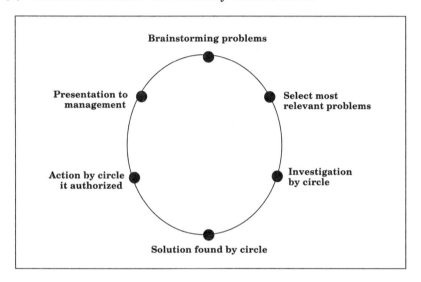

Indeed, as part of any system used by a service or company, QCs will be effective only if they keep open all lines of communication. It should be seen as part of the whole quality programme and can be seen to be effective only if all levels of communication are integrated:

(1) Organisation to outside environment.

(2) Group to group.

(3) Individual to group.

(4) Individual to individual.

Background to Quality Circles

It is surprising to learn that QCs have actually been around since the 1960s. They were first introduced in Japan. In-house training and more responsibility were given to the foreman and operator in industry to spot quality problems. It is thought that there are now over one million QCs in Japanese companies, involving more than 10,000,000 workers.

The Japanese term for quality circles, when translated, is "the gathering of the wisdom of the people."

In the 1970s industry in America also recognised the need for more involvement from the shopfloor and introduced QCs there. It was also introduced as part of the management concept, McGregor Theory Y, and it is important that it is viewed in this way.

During the last few years British companies have also recognised that, to improve quality, the practical way is through participation by the workers.

It could be said that QCs have had a chequered history in the western world. Indeed, five years ago they were being dismissed as just another gimmick. There are several reasons for this:

(1) Management did not discuss with their staff the purpose of QCs or they tried to impose them without consultation and therefore attitudes were all wrong for both parties.

(2) Misunderstanding of the concept created false expectations.

(3) Resistance by management.

(4) Resistance by trade unions.

(5) Empire building by the quality team.

(6) Poor training and no structured programme.

(7) Failure to implement proposals.

(8) Moving too fast, so that it was not possible to deal with all problems.

(9) Team lost interest when they had dealt with "popular" issues.

However, it has been realised that, if the main criteria of having (1) a facilitator, (2) training, (3) management commitment and (4) QC being entirely voluntary , then there is every reason to hope that the QC will be constructive.

It might be useful to mention here that, as well as the four main criteria, the timing of the setting-up of the QC is probably crucial. Attitudes both of management and of staff should be receptive. One chief librarian is very keen on QCs but feels that, as he is in the middle of restructuring at the moment, this should be completed before QCs are requested by supervisors. With supportive management and a structured programme of staff training this should be a natural progression. Management seek a facilitator who can be trained in the necessary skills but also has good enough staff relations to be acceptable to all staff.

Knowsley Careers Service

In 1989 there was a change in part of the funding mechanism for careers services through the Department of Employment Careers Service Branch. Services were required to submit annual plans of work including detailed statistics of the range of work expected to be carried out with clients. This included the number of interviews carried out, the number of group sessions held, industrial visits conducted, clients placed in jobs, etc.

It was felt within Knowsley Careers Service that there was a danger of setting and achieving numerical targets without sufficient regard to the quality of the work being carried out. Having identified the need to evaluate quality as well as quantity, it was felt that QC would be a useful tool in achieving this.

Knowsley Careers Service is run on participative lines on the McGregor Theory Y basis. There is good communication at all levels, such as consultation with all staff on the drawing-up of a statement for the service. It is a people-oriented service; staff support the policies which they have helped to create and they are committed to changes in which they have had a hand.

The progression to using QCs was therefore a logical next step in involving staff in quality issues. Their use is still in the early stages and, to a great extent, staff are using them as a learning experience.

Developing QCs according to the service ethos has been on a very practical basis. The following has been the experience at the Knowsley Community College Careers Office:

Terms of Reference: to spend some time, on a regular basis, examining and discussing aspects of our work, with a view to evaluating the quality.

Participants: all staff wherever possible (allowing for reception and telephone to be staffed).

Procedure: meet once a week for an hour, in groups of varying compositions, depending on the subject for discussion. Wherever possible we aim for a practical outcome.

Initially a variety of topics was covered. Staff now use one session per month to look at the work done with the live register, i.e. clients looking for work, a second session per month to evaluate the Careers Service Management Return on work with clients to Careers Service Branch and any work done in that month on our annual plan. Remaining sessions can then be used to discuss topics which arise through the course of work. Among topics which have been discussed are: information provision, procedures file, evaluation of interviews, work with employers, distribution of work, premises (use of limited space and location), use of "Clips" (information sheets on careers) and computers (problems and needs).

To take an example:

Clips Careers Leaflets

These are being bought from Wiltshire Careers Service under licence; local Knowsley and Merseyside information is being added. They are continually being updated and issued to all schools and careers offices in Knowsley.

Problem: Although staff know of the existence of these leaflets, they were tending not to use them, particularly if the office was busy.

Outcome: The quality circle identified that the reasons they were not being used were:

(1) The sheets were being received on an ongoing basis, which meant that they were not all available at first. This meant that staff used alternative information, which was quicker to hand, if they were busy.

(2)   Often a photocopy would be needed to hand to a client and "Clips" were on the library shelves away from the photocopier.

(3)   Clips leaflets were housed in unwieldy and heavy files.

Solution: Raise staff awareness on the information in Clips by showing them good examples, so that they could see their value; place the Clips volumes next to the photocopier and place multiple copies of the main Clips leaflets in the careers library ready to be handed out.

The quality circle on the use of computers was used not only to identify problems but also to identify items which staff would like to computerise. This is a more complex issue, which needed to be submitted to senior management for any solutions to be implemented. The Clips solutions were fairly simple to implement in-house.

Practical outcomes have been: annual work plans, careers library review, better staff awareness and a feeling of ownership, responsibility and being involved.

Motivation is high as a result and all staff develop and grow professionally. This is reflected in their work.

Initially the QCs were tentative affairs but staff now finds them a useful facility; the input, particularly data collecting, is more structured. Motivation and commitment are fine but there is a feeling that some more constructive training is needed. As already stated, staff are at an early stage in the process and are still learning. These results will be fed back to the facilitator to request the relevant training, so that the motivation and commitment shown are being used properly. The team's recommendations are led back to management and implemented where it is considered necessary.

Warwickshire County Library Service

Philip Gill, the Chief Librarian, and his staff are convinced that the introduction of QCs has been of benefit both to the organisation and those taking part.

Five QCs were established in December 1988 and completed their activities in March 1990. At this point a second series of five was formed and is still active. One of each series has been a workplace circle, the others including members from different libraries in the county. Membership is voluntary and training is provided by a consultant. The QCs choose their own leader, set their own agendas and can present their findings to any level of management, including the library management team. Senior management is committed to the concept and has a contract with the circle ensuring that they receive adequate time for their presentation and that they are informed of action taken as a result.

The teams have addressed issues ranging from detailed procedural matters to the wider issues of communication and training.

Kodak (Merseyside)

Kodak in Merseyside use QCs as a valuable tool in their whole total quality programme. As a subsidiary of a US firm they are somewhat fortunate to have been trained in total quality control and QCs. They have been doing this for the last ten years and as a result have ironed out many of the problems which the rest are usually just encountering. The workforce at this plant is 250.

Senior management have been trained in the United States in performance management and how to "pinpoint", that is identify, problems. Quality-improvement facilitators have been trained on the site and there are now 20 in all. Alan Pendleton, the Senior Facilitator, explained that 70 projects have been undertaken at Kodak and the outcomes have been very worthwhile, particularly in terms of cost. Staff participation has been high in the particular work area from where the natural teams and leader came. Initial opposition from trade unions was overcome by meeting them and giving clear explanations of their use. This had the effect of involving the workforce closely and they could appreciate that the QCs would be run only by volunteers with management only in a listening role.

Problems solved at Kodak were concerned mainly with the assembly lines; for example, high downtime on the assembly line. A multifunctional QC, consisting of not only the staff involved but also engineers, would check the causes and recommend solutions. Not only did it provide a solution but it also made different workers aware of other aspects of the problem.

In 1990 Kodak relaunched QCs by organising them into workshops. In these the same guidelines were used and they found it imperative to get rid of the "crap", i.e. staff concerns, first. All the pet concerns were addressed first, so the voluntary members of the group felt that they and not management were in control. These were addressed along the lines of the six-point plan. So that now, as well as brainstorming problems, they are also addressing new quality issues in their workshops, thus tackling the opportunities as well as the problems. Kodak [is] now using [its] experience in running quality circles to reinforce their total quality programme. Kodak has placed much emphasis on quality and massive resources have gone into their achieving BS5750 18 months ago.

The use of quality circles in organisation can be summed up:

Advantages:

(1) Brings the consideration of quality down to grass-roots level.[2]

(2) Focuses attention on quality as a topic for consideration.

(3) Gives members of staff involved a sense of ownership and involvement.

(4) Develops interpersonal, analytical and leadership skills—also leaders gain respect from members not only in the QC but also in the workplace.

(5) More effective use of resources.

(6) Allows "headroom" for staff development.

(7) Improves team working in the organisation—individual members develop their potential.

Criteria to be met before QCs can be implemented:

(1) A supportive management style which will allow time and resources, and provide relevant facts when needed to the circle.

(2) Good communications between all staff, up, down and across.

(3) Employer and employee relations should be healthy.

(4) Allow time for a programme to develop, realising that it is a long-term commitment.

Factors for success:

(1) Membership should be voluntary.

(2) Top management and operational management support.

(3) A trained facilitator who has sufficient time to devote to the circle.

(4) Training for the leader and members of the team in meeting, problem solving, data collecting and presentation skills.

(5) Shared work background.

(6) Solution-oriented, not just discussing but investigating causes, testing solutions and being involved in solutions.

(7) Recognition from management.

Perhaps it should be mentioned at this point that QCs should not be confused with project groups. These are groups set up by management to tackle a specific problem. Some firms indeed run both project groups and QCs, the main difference being that the project group will contain people from different areas and there is no natural focus and no readily definable house to put in order.

Where Do We Go From Here?

The examples in this article hopefully show that QCs do have a place in the total quality programmes of organisations. It is interesting to see that each of the organisations illustrated reached a point where their original concept of QCs plateaued. However, they have been able to use the learning experiences gained either to start fresh QCs or to seek further training. A change that has been made in larger firms in industry to overcome initial problems has been the appointment of a full-time facilitator to give more time and attention to the running of quality circles. Another has run a course on effective team-building skills to give members a new sense of owning their projects and a third improved internal publicity. Mike Robson[3] in his excellent book on QCs emphasises continually that training is the key together with management commitment and the QC being entirely voluntary. "Training must stick so that the confidence and competence of the group improve in terms of its ability and willingness to tackle its problems."

The National Society for Quality Circles provides a useful pack of information on guidelines to help management and staff in UK organisations to decide if starting a QC programme would be right for them. Among their activities are a national conference for all members to feature presentations and group work; facilitating regional events with member firms; publishing a newsletter and other leaflets; providing a focus for constructive dialogue and co-operation with interested parties both in the UK and abroad; providing advice and contract in member organisations and establishing a library and access to good sources of information on good practice in the UK and abroad.

Libraries are a service organisation and it could be said quality in such organisations can be measured by the interaction between staff and customers. In addressing the changes taking place, quality improvement is becoming a philosophy adopted by organisations in order to survive. In taking this on board the library profession must surely need to address the changes that are taking place from the traditional structures and tailor staff training to them, so that the use of quality circles is a valuable tool in a total quality programme. Increased accountability is becoming the hallmark of all professions. Librarians should be seen to be competent in all management skills and not just in the library issues, or will non-library managers be appointed in future?

For further information please contact: National Society of Quality Circles, 2 Castle Street, Salisbury SP1 1BB. Tel: 0722 26667.

References

1. Morland, J., *Quality Circles*, Industrial Society, London, 1982.

2. McKee, B., *Planning Library Service*, Clive Bingley, London, 1989.

3. Robson, M., *Quality Circles, Gower*, Aldershot, 1982.

Total Quality Management (TQM) in a Hospital Library: Identifying Service Benchmarks

Wenda Webster Fischer, M.S.L.S.

Director, Library / Media Services

Linda B. Reel, M.L.S.

Project Researcher, Library

Alliant Health System

P.O. Box 35070
Louisville, Kentucky 40232

Hospitals are turning to total quality management (TQM) to lower costs of providing care. A hospital library in a TQM environment needs to embrace corporate goals while maintaining its accountability as a contributor to quality patient care. Alliant Health System (AHS) Library at Norton Hospital and Kosair Children's Hospital in Louisville, Kentucky, conducted a study to establish TQM benchmarks and to examine the significance of its role in clinical care. Using a methodology designed to allow both library user and nonuser to respond, 2,091 surveys were distributed to physicians and nursing and allied health personnel. Areas surveyed included frequency of library use, impact of information received on clinical judgments, cognitive value of the information, and satisfaction with library products and services. Results confirm that the library has a substantial clinical role. Eighty-eight percent of reporting physicians agreed that information from the library contributed to higher quality care. Nursing and allied health were less convinced of the importance of the library's clinical role. Sixty-nine percent of nursing personnel and 58 percent of allied health personnel agreed that the library contributed to higher quality care. Nursing and allied health personnel also used the library less frequently than physicians. With these results as benchmarks, improving the clinical role of the library will take commitment to the TQM process and a willingness to change.

Total quality management (TQM) is an approach adopted by hospitals that are anxious to reduce operating expenses created by poor care and wish to provide high-quality care at competitive prices. TQM emphasizes both process and outcome and requires a dramatic shift in many established health care management values and concepts.

TQM is based on the following concepts:

- Change must be based on needs of the customer, not the values of the provider.

- Lack of achievement most likely is caused by system failure rather than by individual performance; therefore, problem solving focuses on the process and joint responsibility rather than on improving individual output.

- Decisions for improvement must come from providers of the service (product) rather than from top managerial authority.

- The emphasis must be on continuous improvement rather than on meeting a specific standard. TQM calls for flexible planning and a climate of continuous change.

The conflict between these concepts and traditional professional autonomy and managerial authority is profound, and it may prove overwhelming for many innovative managers. However, the stakes are high. Industrial organizations that have adopted TQM reportedly have reduced operating expenses by 20 percent to 40 percent; "If health care organizations can do half as well, quality improvement will have a major impact on the field".[1]

Alliant Health System (AHS), which includes three major hospitals in Louisville, Kentucky, is one of many health care systems seeking to monitor and improve the quality of care it provides. AHS has been using and refining its adaptation of TQM since 1986. The AHS Library, which serves two of the three hospitals, undertook a study to determine benchmarks for its present performance.

Purpose of the Study

Recognizing the importance of embracing the corporate quality management program, the AHS Library reviewed how other institutions have incorporated TQM.[2-5] It then undertook a study of customer use and opinion of library products and services, to establish benchmarks of its present performance. In an environment of continuous improvement, benchmarking is critical. The baseline data can be used as a basis of comparison for future improvement and permits comparison with the best of the competition.

The AHS Library chose to emphasize one of its primary missions: the provision of clinical information for the professional staffs of Norton Hospital and Kosair Children's Hospital. This type of activity and studies of how information is provided to medical professionals have been topics of recent interest for many hospital libraries. Several studies have focused on this area, but not all have used exactly the same methodology.[6-9] While this precluded exact comparisons, some indication of AHS's relative status could be derived.

Methodology

The library staff developed a questionnaire with the assistance of the AHS planning and marketing department. Other hospital library surveys were reviewed; some of their survey questions were incorporated, and others were included with revisions. Key topics included frequency of use of AHS Library services, other sources of information used, the impact of library information on clinical judgments, the cognitive value of the information, and customer satisfaction.

Although sampling physicians, the nursing staff, and allied health personnel was considered, the library staff decided that surveying the entire population was not only possible but also desirable as the most statistically reliable and valid approach. Consequently, the entire clinical staff was included. The physician population consisted of active staff, residents, and fellows. Nursing department personnel included registered nurses, licensed practical nurses, and nurses' aides. Allied health was defined as all personnel directly involved in patient care excluding physicians and nursing staff; this group included pharmacists, social workers, respiratory therapists, and laboratory technologists.

Of the 2,101 surveys distributed, 56 percent went to the nursing staff, 23 percent to allied health personnel, and 21 percent to physicians. All participants were accounted for by hospital job code number so that future surveys would duplicate exactly these groups of personnel. This was important in ensuring that future comparisons would be as valid as possible.

The packet of materials included a cover letter, the questionnaire, and a pre-addressed, prestamped return envelope. The cover letter explained the sponsorship and reason for the survey and was signed by the physician chairman of the hospitals' joint library committee. Included was an incentive in the form of a drawing for a $100.00 gift certificate for books. Participants were asked to return a coupon with their completed questionnaire; the winner later was drawn from all returned coupons (which used numbers rather than names to preserve anonymity).

The questionnaire consisted of 11 questions, most of which had between 6 and 9 parts. The document was printed to allow machine-readable tabulation.

The planning and marketing department received the completed surveys and reviewed them for usability, performed the machine tabulation, and compiled the results. This assistance allowed the library staff to maintain distance from the process, to ensure that participants remained anonymous. This division of labor also established the planning and marketing department as a key player in benchmarking products and services of other hospital departments.

Results

Of the 2,101 surveys distributed, 543 usable surveys were returned. This 26 percent response rate qualified to represent the finite population of 2,101 medical professionals.[10] The Z-statistics were computed for a population and for a sample distribution of physician and nonphysician proportions. The Z-statistics (Z-score = 0.93 for the population and 0.93

for the sample distribution) validated the statistical equivalence of these compositions in the sample and population. Estimated margins of error for each subpopulation also were calculated. The computed error of estimation in the total sample of 543 respondents was 3.52 percent (with a finite population correction factor). This error margin was within the generally accepted 5 percent.[11] So the proportions could be generalized to the population of library users within a ±5 percent variation.

Respondents were asked to describe library use as constant (weekly or more), frequent (two or three times a month), occasional (once a month or less), seldom (a few times a year), or never. Overall library usage reflects some of the same patterns reported in other studies.[12-15] Physicians reported using the library more frequently than did nursing and allied health personnel. Eighty percent of the practicing physicians reported using the library either constantly, frequently, or occasionally, and 75 percent of the residents and fellows reported constant, frequent, or occasional use. By contrast, only 40 percent of allied health professionals and 39 percent of the nursing staff reported such usage.

The most conventional services and products listed were the most popular. All categories of users requested journal articles more frequently than any other product or service. Books were the next most heavily used product, again, by all categories of users. For practicing physicians, the third most popular service was MEDLINE† searches conducted by library staff. Residents and fellows preferred conducting their own MEDLINE searches on library equipment. Both allied health and nursing staffs chose audiovisual material as their third most popular service, with MEDLINE searches conducted by library staff ranked fourth.

Respondents did not like performing searches on their own equipment. When describing use of alternative information sources, residents, as well as physicians and nurses, ranked searching on their own computer last. For physicians, residents, fellows, and nurses, the most frequently used source of information was their own private library, followed by the AHS Library. Allied health users chose the AHS Library first, then their own libraries. The third most frequently used source for all users was the local network of professional colleagues. The complete set of data is presented in Table 1.

The survey relied on historical use of the library to evaluate the impact of information on clinical judgment. Physicians, residents, and fellows were asked how often information received through library services affected their judgments related to diagnosis, diagnostic tests, choice of drugs, choice of other therapy, and length of patient stay.

Over 50 percent of the practicing physicians reported that the information affected their clinical judgments relating to diagnosis, choice of drugs, and choice of other therapy. Forty-eight percent indicated that it affected choice of diagnostic tests. Residents and fellows gave similar responses; however, 63 percent reported an effect on choice of diagnostic tests, and 52 percent reported an effect on choice of other therapy. Both practicing physicians and residents/fellows reported a lesser impact on length of patient stay (17 percent and 15 percent, respectively).

Table 1
Information source preference by professional affiliation

Rank of total sample	Information source	Total		Physician		Resident/fellow		Nurse		Allied health	
		Average score	No. of cases	Average score	No. of cases	Average score	No. of cases	Average score	No. of cases	Average score	No. of cases
1	Private library	3.29	506	2.07	85	2.42	36	3.53	215	3.80	170
2	AHS Library	3.50	502	2.73	81	2.60	35	3.78	212	3.70	174
3	Local colleague network	3.75	497	3.43	82	3.14	35	3.81	211	3.98	169
4	Have assistant do information gathering	4.21	485	3.85	79	4.15	33	4.26	207	4.33	166
5	University medical library	4.23	500	3.76	83	4.09	35	4.29	213	4.43	169
6	National colleague network	4.25	496	3.90	82	4.17	35	4.33	211	4.34	168
7	Hospital library other than AHS	4.50	492	4.27	82	4.35	34	4.56	209	4.57	167
8	Other	4.65	137	3.88	8	4.00	4	4.72	64	4.72	61
9	Search with own computer	4.71	500	4.64	83	4.69	36	4.80	213	4.63	168

Score scale: 1 = constant; 5 = never

Nursing and allied health providers were asked how often library information affected patient classification, patient assessment, research on diagnosis, provision of patient education, and development of new services. Both nursing and allied health personnel indicated that the information had the greatest effect on research for diagnosis and patient education and the least effect on patient classification.

Asked how library information made a difference in clinical decisions, practicing physicians and residents/fellows either strongly agreed or agreed that it contributed to higher quality care (88 percent and 83 percent, respectively). The information refreshed their memory (89 percent and 92 percent) and contained some knowledge that was new to them (74 percent and 89 percent). Although over half of nursing and allied health respondents also strongly agreed or agreed that information provided contributed to high-quality care, they were less convinced than the physicians (69 percent of nursing and 58 percent of allied health). This pattern held for providing new information (69 percent nursing and 62 percent allied health). These data are presented in Table 2.

Table 2

Strongly agree and agree that information received from the library has clinical value

	Physician No. (%)	Resident No. (%)	Nurse No. (%)	Allied health No. (%)
Cognitive value				
Refreshes memory	72 (89%)	33 (92%)	138 (67%)	103 (62%)
Some new knowledge	58 (74%)	31 (89%)	138 (69%)	103 (62%)
Substantiates prior knowledge	42 (55%)	22 (67%)	105 (53%)	64 (40%)
Contribution to quality care				
Contributes to higher quality care	72 (88%)	30 (83%)	139 (69%)	96 (58%)
Contributes to better clinical decisions	66 (85%)	27 (79%)	131 (65%)	98 (60%)

The library collection and library staff were the final areas evaluated. Question topics ranged from knowledge and cooperation of staff to convenience of location and hours. The responses regarding overall quality of service and information are detailed in Figure 1. The highest ratings for both staff and information came from practicing physicians.

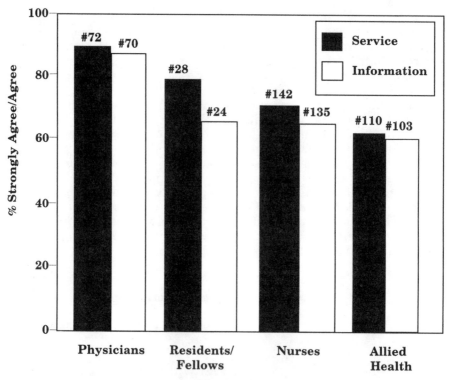

Fig. 1. Strongly agree/agree that library service and library information are excellent.

Discussion

One of the differences between this survey and previous customer surveys at AHS was the inclusion of the entire population of potential clinical users. This was important not only because it established statistical validity but also because it captured the responses of infrequent users and nonusers. Analysis of this full spectrum of data revealed that constant, frequent, or occasional users were more likely to believe the library made a positive contribution to quality care. Conversely, those who seldom or never used the library were more likely to have no opinion or a negative opinion of the library's contribution.

Furthermore, unlike the King study, which reported no correlation between frequency of library use and perception of clinical value of library information,[16] this study found a clear link. For example, compared to physicians, lower percentages of nursing and allied health personnel used the library frequently, and correspondingly, lower percentages found the information useful in making clinical judgments. In addition, a lower percentage of nursing and allied health personnel thought the library made a contribution to quality care (Figure 2).

From a traditional marketing point of view, these correlations suggest that the library needs to increase use of its resources to improve its image as a contributor to quality care and as a useful tool for making clinical judgments. But TQM calls for a more complex examination. Should library resources be used to increase library use by the health professional who derives limited clinical value? Is infrequent usage due to the library's failure to meet information needs? Or is it due to a diminished need for a variety of published information sources?

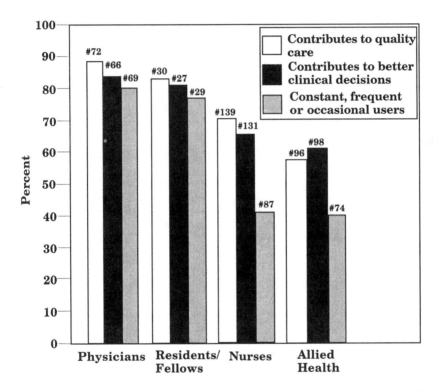

Fig. 2. Comparison of library usage and opinion of its contribution to quality care and better clinical decisions.

The answers to these questions may clash with the traditional views that a library should service all who have the intellectual curiosity to enter its doors and that the more knowledge an individual has the better job that individual can do. However, within the context of TQM, the unsettling possibility of such a clash could lead to positive change. Because the driving force in TQM is customer needs rather than provider values, the AHS Library must probe deeply, through focus groups and individual contacts, to establish its proper role in providing clinical information to all, particularly to nursing and allied health personnel. Definition of this role is complicated by the fact that provision of clinical information is only one of the library missions. If fewer resources were devoted to clinical information for nursing and allied health personnel, then what resources should be provided to this group in terms of nonclinical information support?

Because the provision of clinical information is among the library's primary missions, it is satisfying that the survey results show that physicians not only use the library but also believe the clinical information contributes to higher quality care. Fortunately, in this case, the needs of the customer coincide with the values of the provider. However, in adopting continuous improvement as a legitimate goal, the library pledges to improve its high rating from physicians. One possible approach is to target physicians who seldom use information from the library to modify or confirm clinical judgments. One particular medical specialty was over-represented in this group of users. The library staff plan to meet with physicians in this specialty to find out how library information could be made more useful in development of clinical judgments.

Conclusion

This survey provided internal baseline data and identified important areas for further internal investigation. It did not, however, provide data enabling direct comparison with other libraries. More specifically, the AHS study confirmed other studies showing that clinical information from the library does affect clinical judgment. The methodology popular in other studies, which was based on current rather than historical library use, may have presented more accurate pictures of how clinical information affects clinical judgment. However, this approach gathers responses only from library users. The AHS study was designed not only to determine whether library information made an impact on clinical judgment, but also to gather data to improve library performance. For this purpose, the approach of gathering information from the infrequent user and the nonuser was as important as surveying more frequent users. By relying on historical use of the library, AHS captured the infrequent user and nonuser response, although comparisons with other libraries were compromised.

This leaves issues that require further exploration. If true national benchmarks are to be established, standard baseline criteria and survey instruments must be created for interlibrary studies.

Two other areas that require further attention are evaluation of service areas most useful to allied health and nursing personnel and development of library resources to meet these customers' needs, and research to learn why some physicians, residents, and fellows did not find the clinical information provided useful and how library services could be improved to accommodate them.

Overall, this study established benchmarks of frequency of library use. It assessed the clinical value of information provided to users, and it evaluated the performance of library staff and the quality of service. The library staff now must use this knowledge effectively in other phases of TQM. Success will depend on commitment and willingness to change.

Acknowledgments

This study was made possible through a $5,000 Community Trust Grant from AHS, Louisville, Kentucky.

Special thanks are extended to the Joint Library Committee of Kosair Children's Hospital and Norton Hospital; Neal Smith, marketing manager, planning and marketing department, AHS; and Sukhen Dey, Ph.D., associate professor of Computing Science, Indiana University SE, New Albany, Indiana.

For more complete information on any aspect of the study or for a copy of the survey, contact Wenda Webster Fischer at 17200 Creek Ridge Road, Louisville, Kentucky 40245-4358.

References

1. McLaughlin CP, Kalunzy AD. Total quality management in health: making it work. Health Care Manage Rev 1990 Summer;15(3):7-14.

2. Ibid.

3. Berwick DM. Sounding board: continuous improvement as an ideal in health care. NEJM 1989 Jan 5;320(1):53-6.

4. Fredenburg AM. Quality assurance; establishing a program for special libraries. Spec Libr 1988 Fall;79(4):277-83.

5. Buchanan HS. Total quality management: an introductory course for librarians. 2d ed. (Course guide for MLA New Perspectives course 211.) Louisville, Kentucky, 1991.

6. King DN. The contribution of hospital library information services to clinical care: a study in eight hospitals. Bull Med Libr Assoc 1987 Oct;75(4):291-301.

7. Medical Library Association Hospital Library Section, Medical Library Association Library Research Section. Symposium: evaluation in health sciences libraries: measuring our contribution and our value [guide for symposium during the Eighty-ninth Annual meeting of the Medical Library Association, May 25, 1989]. Chicago, IL: the Association, 1989.

8. Gilbert CM, Manko D. Evaluation of library information services. Nat Network 1990;14(3):13-25.

9. Marshall JG. The impact of the hospital library on clinical decision making: the Rochester study. Bull Med Libr Assoc 1992;80(2):169-84.

10. Brightman H, Schneider H. Statistics for business problem solving. Cincinnati: South-Western Publishing Company, 1992:320-432.

11. Ingram JA. Introductory statistics. Menlo Park, CA: Cummings Publishing Company, 1974.

12. Marshall, op. cit.

13. Gilbert, op. cit.

14. Medical Library Association Hospital Library Section, op. cit.

15. King, op. cit.

16. Ibid., 300.

Libraries Around Australia: Introducing Total Quality Management in Telecom's National Resource Centre

Barbara Armstrong

Prior to joining Telecom, Barbara Armstrong worked in the health field for twenty years. She has worked as Manager of the Information Management Advisory Section of the Health Department of Victoria, as Microcomputer Systems Consultant for a computer software company, and ran her own medical record consultancy business. Barbara has had extensive experience with the analysis, design and implementation of manual and computerised systems. Her current position with Telecom is National Quality Manager. Barbara has qualifications in medical record administration, computing, and library and information science.

In June 1990, Telecom Australia's National Information Resource Centre took the initiative of creating a new position of National Quality Assurance Co-ordinator. This paper describes the Quality Assurance Co-ordinator's initial steps in introducing Total Quality Management within information services. The author points out that there is more to quality management than the use of statistical tools. However, many of these techniques can be translated from the field of manufacturing and successfully used in the field of information management.

Starting Out on the Road to Quality

The National Information Resource Centre was established in July 1988 to provide Telecom Australia with superior and enhanced information services and products which are directly linked to its business aims and objectives: to manage information as a strategic resource in a competitive business environment.[1] The Centre (usually known as the NIRC) has fifty staff who provide services from six locations—at Perth, Brisbane, Adelaide, Sydney, the Corporate Center in the central business district of Melbourne, and the headquarters at Telecom Research Laboratories in Clayton, Victoria.

Telecom Australia has a keen interest in improving the quality of its services and is in the process of implementing Total Quality Management (TQM) as a vital management tool throughout the organisation. To implement

(This article was first published in *The Australian Library Journal* 40 (4) November 1991. Reprinted, with permission of the Australia Library and Information Association.)

this goal, senior management of Telecom's National Information Resource Centre created a new position of National Quality Manager. The author commenced work in this position in June 1990. This paper describes her approach to the introduction of Total Quality Management within Telecom's National Information Resource Centre.

First Steps

It soon became clear that many staff were unclear about the scope of activities involved with quality management and the role of the Quality Manager. Some thought the position was solely to do with gathering statistics, while others thought it was related to the in-house computer system. These misconceptions were understandable because of the way the advertisement for the position had been worded, and the emphasis on statistical methods and tools in TQM publications. Most of the literature on TQM is related to the manufacturing industry and gives manufacturing examples—for example, how to use statistical tools to measure the size, strength, content, or variability of products.

However, there are many aspects to quality management, all of which are important for a balanced quality program. There has been a tendency by some to concentrate on only a few aspects, such as statistics and economics, and consider them sufficient.[2] Experience has shown that 'quality managers in service organizations are less apt to deal with sophisticated statistical techniques and more apt to deal with evasive data such as the emotional content of customer complaints or empathy shown by an employee.'[3]

The first two initiatives undertaken by the Quality Manager were aimed at helping to clarify the meaning and purpose of TQM, and the role of the Quality Manager and all staff in making quality improvements.

One initiative was to produce and circulate a paper to all staff, explaining the philosophy of quality assurance and its application to information management and the NIRC.[4] It included the criteria by which users measure services. Clients want services which are:

- accessible

- timely

- accurate, up-to-date and relevant

- non-threatening, friendly and helpful

- easy to use or operate

- consistent and reliable

- within their price range.

The paper also listed questions which service providers should ask themselves when trying to identify opportunities for improvement, namely:

- What factors inhibit the accessibility of our services?

- What processes create delays?

- Is the information that we provide accurate, up-to-date and relevant? How do we know? Can it be improved?

- Do our contacts with our clients leave them with a feeling of having received good service—even if they left with nothing? Will they want to return? Would they want to recommend us to their work mates?

- Have we done everything we can to make it easy for them to negotiate their way through our information world? Can we reduce the complexity of the system or of the products we produce?

- Can we assure them that their dealings with us are private and confidential?

- Is each product and service consistent and reliable in terms of quality, timeliness, etc.? Can clients rely on us?

- Can we identify areas where costs can be reduced? Are there any areas of waste?

This paper was followed by a more informal letter to the State Managers of the NIRC, which pointed out that, in service industries like Telecom, all tasks require technical and people skills, and that a good balance of both is required to provide quality service to external clients and to workmates (our 'internal clients'). Therefore, the role of the Quality Manager requires involvement in both the technical and people aspects of quality.

The second initiative was to take steps to improve the staff induction process. Effective staff induction is seen as being an important factor in achieving the first of Deming's famous fourteen points—'create constancy of purpose'.[5] While being an important issue in its own right, it also achieved the purpose of indicating to staff that quality management has broader implications than just statistical tools and computer systems. Standard checklists and guidelines for staff induction have been created for each group (i.e., cataloguing, acquisitions, information services) so that all relevant topics are routinely covered with every new staff member, from the perspective of that group.

Getting to Know the Business

High on the list of priorities was the need to discover how the NIRC operated and what opportunities for improvement were immediately identifiable.

Two main ways in which opportunities for improvement can be identified are:

- input from clients, for example, surveys of client perceptions of the quality of products and services;

- input from staff, for example, surveys of staff perceptions and suggestions.

The second option was chosen because the Quality Manager was new to the organisation and because it was considered important to involve staff in problem identification and the problem-solving process at an early stage. It recognises that the identification of quality improvements is everyone's responsibility, not just that of the Quality Manager.

Interviews were conducted with staff. A questionnaire was issued to each person a week before they were interviewed. The questionnaire used as prompts those quality criteria by which clients evaluate services, and which had already been explained in the paper issued to all staff. The preliminary questionnaire provided the opportunity for staff to prepare themselves and focus on the issues. The discussion allowed them to add context to the issues raised. Results were amalgamated, grouped under common themes, and documented in a report to the appropriate section manager.

The Issues

Identified issues related to such things as documentation, training, communication, project management and time delays. There was a long list of problems and suggestions, some of which could be classified as relatively minor causes of irritation (significant because of their ongoing nature and their ability to 'niggle' and aggravate), while others had major implications for the people involved and ultimately for the NIRC as a whole (and therefore its clients).

Identification of these issues led to the development of two projects to begin a process of improvement. The choice was influenced by Juran's recommendation that initial projects:

- address a chronic problem—one that has been awaiting solution for a long time;

- are feasible—likely to achieve results within a few months;

- are significant—will merit attention and recognition;

- are measurable.[6]

To this list was added the need to have a favourable reception, with an enthusiastic group, rather than be likely to meet resistance.

Cataloguing Data Input

One of the identified opportunities was the need to streamline the process of inputting catalogue records to the in-house computer system.

It would be very easy to alter the computer programs and rely on 'gut feeling' after the event to assess whether the changes had or had not been successful. However, with any 'enhancements' to systems there is always potential for disagreement regarding the effectiveness of those changes. Therefore the project was set up to provide a quantitative assessment of whether the programming changes to the data input procedures had, in fact, streamlined the process by saving time. To do this it was necessary to take a before and after 'snap-shot' of the computer data entry part of the cataloguing process, and compare the two to see what difference, if any, the changes made to the process.

Two types of 'snapshots' were taken: the stages required for cataloguers to input data for a new item were flow charted before and after the programming changes, and a series of timings of before and after how long it took to input catalogued data into the computer were made. These timings were recorded on average, and range, statistical control charts.

Obviously there will be some variation in the amount of time it takes to input data into a system, even if it is the same kind of data being entered each time. However, the data entry time will remain within a predictable range, unless the process is altered, for example by improving training, hardware or software. Statistical control charts are useful tools to display the normal variation in a process, and the results of changes to the process.

Originally the data entry part of the cataloguing process was very cumbersome. Naturally, the cataloguers hoped the changes would reduce the steps in the flow chart, indicating a simplification and streamlining of the process, and thus reduce the amount of time required for data entry.

The two snapshots proved the desired results had been achieved: Six steps and three potential error paths had been pruned from the flow chart. The statistical control charts also showed a significant drop in both the average and the range of time to input catalogued data into the computer.

Throughout the project the team used what is known as the PDCA cycle:

- Plan—determine the issues, objectives, strategies, action plan, checks and measures;

- Do—train, carry out the plan (or a pilot), gather data;

- Check—check the progress versus plan, the results versus objectives, any waste or rework;

- Act—standardise good solutions, improve the plan, or cut losses;

- Then start the PDCA cycle again.

Interlibrary Loans

Interlibrary loans was also identified as an area where the use of TQM tools could be tested. Similar steps to those previously described are being taken. In addition to using flow charts to document the workflow, cause and effect diagrams have been used to brainstorm ideas. Frequency diagrams, run charts and boxplots are also being used to document the work volume and the time to complete each stage in the process.

The boxplot (sometimes referred to as a 'box and whisker plot') is not one of the standard tools of TQM. However, it is a useful way to provide a graphical summary of a histogram, and to display a summary of a series of histograms over time. Each boxplot shows:

- the extent of the distribution (the whiskers extending from the ends of the box)

- the median (the central line in the box)

- the upper and lower quartiles (the ends of the box)

- individual points beyond the whiskers which are possibly atypical

- the mean (represented as an asterisk).

Therefore the one boxplot, such as that shown, can graphically display information such as the following:

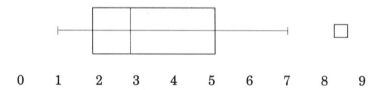

During June:

- 25% of items were returned within, say, 2 days

- 50% were returned within 5 days

- 75% were returned within 7 days

- the earliest time was 1 day

- the latest time was 10 days

- on average most items were returned within x days.

A series of boxplots shows performance over time.

The aim of the project and of the tools mentioned above is to assess the issues involved, and determine appropriate actions and their effect.

For example, the monitoring process helped the project team identify and remedy a gap in the procedure for handling requests when staff members were away for long periods. The project should also help staff give clients a clearer idea of the likely delivery date of material.

Conclusion

The quality issues which are tackled in service organisations are extremely broad and involve both the people and technical aspects of service delivery. Statistical techniques form only part of the toolkit of Quality Managers, and should not dominate their thinking. Many of these techniques can be translated from the field of manufacturing and for successful use in the field of information management.

At Telecom's National Information Resource Centre the first steps have been taken to implement and use the tools of Total Quality Management. The National Quality Manager is working in conjunction with staff to review the NIRC's products, services, systems and training, and to monitor and evaluate the development and implementation of initiatives for improvement.

References

1. Helen V. Rodd, The National Information Resource Centre in Telecom Australia; An overview, September 1989, Melbourne. 1989.

2. A. C. Rosander, *The quest for quality in services,* Quality Press, Milwaukee, Wisconsin, 1989.

3. Carol A. King, 'Service quality assurance is different', *Quality Progress,* June 1985, pp. 14-18.

4. Barbara Armstrong, 'Quality assurance and the NIRC', *NIRC Paper No. 5*, Melbourne, June 1989.

5. W. Edwards Deming, *Out of the crisis: quality, productivity and competitive position*, Cambridge University Press, Melbourne, 1986.

6. J. M. Juran, *Juran on Leadership for Quality: an Executive Handbook*, Free Press, New York, 1988.

Just Another Management Fad? The Implications of TQM for Library and Information Services

John R. Brockman

Librarian
Ministry of Defence Libraries (Bromley)

Paper presented to the 34th Annual Conference of the Electronics Group, Danbury Park Management Centre, Chelmsford, 14-16 May 1992.

Abstract

The quality issue represents one of the greatest challenges facing managers in the 1990s. This paper presents an overview of the development of quality management in library and information services (LIS) on the basis of its evolution from quality control, through quality assurance (QA), to total quality management (TQM). This development is exemplified by case studies of UK and North American LIS which have been required to comply with quality strategies of their parent organizations, and those which have adopted unilateral strategies.

The literature of quality management seems rife with confusion over terminology. Some of this appears to have been the result of the so-called "quality gurus" asserting the novelty of their individual philosophies of quality. Each is followed by a band of disciples and devotees (consultants and other practitioners) who are equally keen to promote their own particular approaches to quality management and sometimes add to the terminological morass. As well as the conventional terms defined below, we also find Total Quality Control, Total Quality Assurance, Quality Assurance and Service Reliability, Company Wide Quality Control, Marketing Quality Assurance, Quality Service, Service Quality and so on.

For present purposes the standard BSI/ISO definitions will be adopted for the three most common, and most frequently confused, concepts.[1] These are as follows:

Quality control: The operational techniques and activities that are used to fulfill requirements for quality. Quality control ... aims both at monitoring a process and at eliminating causes of unsatisfactory performance at relevant stages of the quality loop in order to result in economic effectiveness.

Quality assurance (QA): All those planned and systematic actions necessary to provide adequate confidence that a product or service will satisfy given requirements for quality.

Total quality management (TQM): A management philosophy embracing all activities through which the needs of the customer and the community, and the objectives of the organization are satisfied in the most efficient and cost effective way by maximizing the potential of all employees in a continuing drive for improvement.

It should be noted that TQM embodies the first two, together with all other management activities. Burgess,[2] sees them as the final phases in the evolution of quality management, in which the steps are:

- craftsmanship

- the Industrial Revolution

- mass production

- inspection

- quality control

- quality assurance

- total quality management

An analysis of the management literature of the last ten years provides an insight into the growth of interest in TQM, and is perhaps indicative of its rate of take-up (see Figure 1). The fact that the exponential growth of the TQM literature begins in about 1988, the point at which the growth of the QA literature tends to flatten out, suggests that this could be the cross-over point in the evolution of QA into TQM. For the sake of clarity the progress of the quality control literature has been omitted. As a much older technique its use is more widespread and yields about 800 publications a year, and is still slowly rising. This graph also charts the decline of the somewhat disparaged quality circles approach to quality management, of which more will be said later.

By comparison, the literature of library and information science up to 1990 suggests that practitioners in this area were still not taking the quality management revolution very seriously (see Figure 2). Unfortunately the 1991 input has been very slow to get into the two databases used as the source for this analysis.

As organizations have progressed towards TQM the most important changes involve the roles of management and measurement. In the case of the former, the responsibility for quality ceases to be delegated to QA staff and becomes the concern of all employees, but especially top management. The emphasis of measurement systems also changes from being internally to externally oriented and more customer-focused. In the TQM environment an increasingly important measurement technique is benchmarking, which has been defined as: ... the continuous process of measuring products, services, and practices against the toughest competitors, or those companies recognized as industry leaders.[3]

Annual number of publications

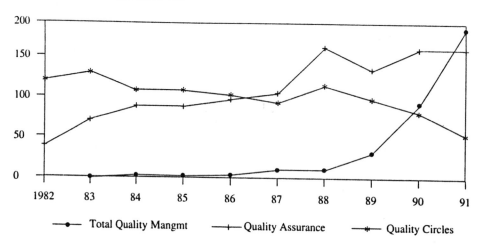

Source: ABI/INFORM database

Fig. 1. The management literature.

Annual number of publications

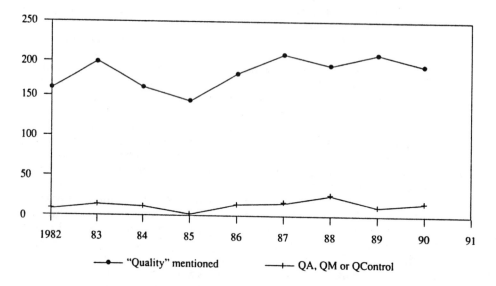

Source: LISA and Inf. ScI. Abs. database

Fig. 2. The library and information science literature.

Many library managers are quite accustomed to making comparisons using the various library statistical compilations. Inter-library comparison has tended, however, to concentrate on mean values of performance indicators, rather than identifying the leading performers as a spur to achieving excellence.

Quality Control

In view of the above developmental sequence it seems significant that one of the earliest general discussions of the management of quality in library and information services (LIS) dealt with this matter at the quality control level. In 1988 O'Neill and Vizine-Goetz of the Online Computer Library Center (OCLC) described methods of quality control in the online information industry, and traced this activity back to the 1960s when work started on the development of the theory and methods of automatically detecting and correcting spelling errors and applying self-checking numbers to machine-readable data.[4] These authors also review the methods of authority control to ensure consistency in the form of headings used in bibliographical records, and correcting or supplying punctuation and capitalization, as well as detecting duplicate records.

A recent survey of the online industry seems to suggest that some hosts, and many producers, are still focusing primarily on quality control, with its emphasis on checking, inspection and proof-reading, rather than on the broader more externally-oriented process of quality management.[5] There are exceptions, and Dialog Information Service, Inc., sees customer feedback as essential in "closing the loop in the quality assurance circle".[6] It has been largely through the recent efforts of the Library Association and the UK Online User Group that representatives of the online industry and users have now come together to discuss the broader aspects of quality of these services.[7]

Quality Assurance

One of the most significant phrases in the above BSI/ISO definition of QA is "given requirements", for this implies the provision of goods and services in accordance with a *published standard* recognized and accepted by both the producer and customer.

If we move up to the quality assurance level we therefore find that those LIS involved fall into two broad categories:

- Services whose parent organizations have obtained certification under the British Standards Institution standard on quality assurance, BS5750/ISO 9000.

- Services which have initiated their own approach to QA, and perhaps may even seek quality certification on their own account.

There are probably more LIS in the first category than the literature would suggest, but one of the few published accounts of the processes involved is that of the Senior Librarian of the Building Design Partner-ship (BDP).[8] The parent company recognized the business advantages to be gained by achieving national and international recognition within the design profession as a firm of assessed quality. Most importantly, BDP would receive an entry in the DTI's published register of quality-assessed organizations. As with all such cases, BDP was required to demonstrate to the BS5750 auditors that it had established and maintained procedures to control all documents (standards, specifications and manuals) relating to the requirements of the QA standard. This led to a raising of the level of recognition of BDP's Information Centres, accompanied by an increase in their funding and launching of additional services. The company acknowledged that certification could not have been achieved without being able to produce evidence of adequate information services.

Turning to the second group, one of the most notable examples are the Canadian medical libraries, which must be regarded as the pioneers of LIS QA. As early as 1967 medical staff library services became a prerequisite under the Canadian Council on Health Facilities Accreditation Scheme.[9] Since then medical library standards have been extended and refined and they now take into account: library goals and objectives; organization and administration; direction and staffing; facilities, equipment and supplies; policies and procedures; information resources and services; education; and QA systems. Qualitative guidelines were also produced for each of these eight sets of descriptive standards, which in 1989 were being revised in order to emphasize outcome measures and risk management.

An interesting UK case involves the Taywood Information Service, part of the Taylor Woodrow group, which successfully applied for certification under BS5750, the first LIS to do so on its own account.[10] Like the BDP Information Centres, Taywood Information Service was already involved with a succession of quality audits conducted in connection with the certifi-cation of the various Taylor Woodrow companies forming its customer base.

Taywood Information Service saw certification not only as a means of reducing the number of audits, but also considered that a fully-fledged quality system would form a useful management tool. Most importantly of all, its registration sent a vital message to senior management that it was doing a top-rate job, important when money was short.

One consideration when planning possible quality strategies concerns the choice between certification under BS5750, and aiming at full-scale TQM. The difference is largely one of scope, and the choice depends on whether management feels that quality can best be improved by installing quality systems, or whether a cultural change is called for. This question has been addressed by several general writers on TQM, and at least one information science academic.[11]

Total Quality Management

As explained above, TQM incorporates QA as one of its elements, but even the experts disagree on whether an organization should seek BS5750 QA certification before embarking on TQM, or vice versa.

When considering this relationship between QA and TQM it is instructive to examine the experience of the Information Services of ICI Chemicals and Polymers Ltd.[12] This company, in partnership with a number of others in the ICI Group, saw TQM as a means of achieving a very necessary cultural shift which would lead to a new form of supplier/customer relationship in which internal as well as external customers would be recognized.

Following initial TQM training, the main thrust changed to QA; TQM determined the requirements and QA assured that they were met. The company's Information Services now has it own QA manager in order to satisfy the conditions of BS5750, and has found that as well as clear benefits to its customers, major cost savings are achievable from the closer definition of requirements.

As in the case of QA, LIS which have embarked on TQM fall into two main groups: those whose parent organizations are adopting TQM and the LIS are therefore required to follow general policy, as in the case of ICI, and those which are doing so unilaterally on their own initiative.

When examining those in the first category it is particularly appropriate to look at the case of the corporate library serving Florida Power & Light (FPL), a public utility providing electricity to about half the state of Florida. FPL is notable for being the first, and so far only, non-Japanese company to win the world's most coveted and prestigious quality award, the Deming Prize of Japan. The latter was named in honour of Dr. Edwards Deming, the American quality expert who in Japan is regarded as a national hero for his contribution to Japan's post-war reconstruction.

One of the many published accounts of FPL's success story describes two of the library-related implications of this achievement, and particularly the team approach to the identification of quality problems and their elimination.[13] One of the library teams established improved procedures for processing requests for items not in stock. This was not a complex problem, but it helped library staff to learn the process, from problem identification, to preventing the problem and its root causes from recurring, to final evaluation of the team's effectiveness. The second problem area involved the provision of library and information services to remote locations of the FPL system using a cross-functional team approach to address the various logistical problems, with members drawn from both library staff and customers. Publicizing quality achievements is important in TQM, and in FPL this was done by means of team "storyboards" displayed in hallways illustrating the problem-solving process undertaken by each team. (The names adopted by the two library teams sound whimsical to British ears: The Clippers and The Happy Bookers!)

It is interesting, and perhaps significant, that those LIS which have been actively involved in their parent organization's TQM strategy appear to have become very integrated into the functioning of the organization. In the case of the Weyerhauser Company, a leading US wood-products manufacturer, the LIS became responsible for the corporate Center for

Quality Resources, a vital component of the company's drive for quality.[14] This recognition was aided by a benchmarking survey, of the type described above, in collaboration with similar LIS.

The second category of LIS under this heading, those which have adopted TQM on their own account, inevitably contains large monolithic services, such as the US Defense Technical Information Center (DTIC) and the National Technical Information Service (NTIS).

DTIC is the central point within the Department of Defense (DoD) for acquiring, storing, retrieving and disseminating scientific and technical information to support the management and conduct of DoD R&D programmes. It has a staff of just under 400. DTIC's mission statement includes the pursuit of a programme for applying advanced techniques and technologies for developing improvements in services and in information transfer effectiveness. The formal adoption of TQM within DTIC is a relatively recent development, but this objective occupies second place in the organization's eight-point vision statement for the year 2000.

One of the first components of DTIC's quality strategy, pre-dating TQM by several years, was the staff suggestions scheme. Suggestions are known locally as Model Installation Proposals (MIPs). These have been the source of many good ideas, and rewards range from on-the-spot cash awards of up to $250, to a 'pat on the back'. The MIP scheme is open to DTIC's users (including DoD contractors) as well as its own staff, but the former are not eligible for cash awards. During the author's recent visit the DTIC Administrator mentioned that the number of suggestions is declining, but so much has been accomplished through the scheme that he considered that such a fall-off is inevitable.

The second step in the evolution of the strategy was the introduction of quality circles (QCs), in which about one quarter of the staff currently participate. The composition of QCs cuts across organizational divisions and hierarchies, and their number fluctuates as quality-related problems arise, and then are solved. There is also a QC of QC leaders, forming an inner circle, and once a year DTIC holds a QC Recognition Day. The proportion of staff involved in QCs has recently declined, but once again the Administrator did not regard this as significant, and thought it could even be regarded as an encouraging sign.

In 1989, after working with the MIP scheme and QCs, DTIC's quality strategy evolved into comprehensive TQM, managed by a full-time TQM Coordinator. Its implementation embraces the principles and supports the goals of the TQM Master Plan of the Defense Logistics Agency, DTIC's parent body, and its development is the responsibility of a TQM Executive Steering Committee chaired by the Deputy Administrator. An annual one-week user conference is an important feature of DTIC's quality strategy.

Like DTIC, the TQM strategy of NTIS, a similarly-sized body, evolved from the use of QCs coupled with a well-established staff suggestions scheme. NTIS TQM is controlled by a full-time manager and a full-time QC facilitator, while policy is formulated by a Quality Management Council chaired by the Head of NTIS. QCs, which currently number nine, are employee-operated and comprise five to ten members, usually meeting once a week. Each circle contains a trade union representative. During these sessions problems are brainstormed and data collected, and if necessary the circle can call for supporting research and other resources to help with solutions. Currently about 80 percent of QC proposals are accepted by NTIS management. With the advent of TQM in NTIS the emphasis of group problem-solving shifted to wider areas of concern than those of the QCs, and newly formed groups represented both employees and management. TQM implementation included an employee survey of attitudes to quality, and questionnaire surveys of customers are regularly undertaken.

In 1987 NTIS received the US Senate Productivity Award for Virginia for its innovative use of automation, QCs, improved communication, professional development and integrated planning systems to improve productivity.

Conclusion

Returning to the question posed in the title of this paper, is TQM another management fad? Currently there is no evidence to suggest any fall-off in its application, in spite of its very high failure rate. One authority estimates this to be as high as 80 per cent of all TQM programmes,[15] and even Florida Power & Light is now revamping its quality programme in favour of an approach which places more emphasis on communication.[16] One complaint is that private sector TQM has frequently been slow in producing bottomline results, and that its emphasis on processes has sometimes produced excessive bureaucracies.

There have also been misconceptions on the part of many managements about the scope for TQM. The word "total" refers of course to "management", and not to "quality". This give rise to assumption that TQM can only be implemented across an entire organization, and not to an individual part or parts, such as an LIS. This is not the case, and as the quality guru Philip Crosby claims, a unit within an organization *can* implement TQM on its own, and if effective, others will want to know the remedy for its success. He calls such initiators 'quality heros'.[17]

Furthermore, one of the four new Civil Service College courses on TQM focuses on its introduction into a small organization or section,[18] and figures as low as 50 employees have been quoted as indicative of the smallest firm which could possibly benefit from introduction of TQM.[19]

Several UK associations for information professionals have recently held courses and seminars on QA. There now appears to be a need to make LIS managers aware of how their services can benefit from operating in the broader TQM environment, and how they can best respond to the implementation of TQM by their parent organizations. This potential has now been recognized by the US Special Libraries Association and Council on Library Resources, who are sponsoring a travelling continuing education course on TQM for librarians.[20]

References

1. British Standards Institution. *Quality vocabulary: Part 2, concepts and related definitions.* (BS 4778: Part 2: 1991.)

2. Burgess, N. The theory of quality assurance. *In* Brockman, J. R. Quality assurance (QA) and the management of information services: A one-day seminar organized jointly by the Institute of Information Scientists and Task Force Pro Libra, Ltd. and held on the 7th November 1990. [Seminar report] *Journal of Information Science* 17, 1991. pp.127-135.

3. Camp, R. C. *Benchmarking: the search for industry best practices that lead to superior performance.* Milwaukee, Wis.: Quality Press, 1989. p.10.

4. O'Neill, E. T. *and* Vizine-Goetz, D. Quality control in online data-bases. *Annual Review of Information Science* 23 1988, pp. 125-156.

5. Focus: online hosts and quality assurance; database providers and quality assurance. *Information World Review* (63) November 1991, pp. 24-25.

6. Day, J. Quality management: UKOLUG annual lecture, IOLIM 91. [report] *UK Online User Group Newsletter* 3 (1) 1992, pp. 2-3.

7. Day, J.

8. Dawes, S. The impact of BS5750 on library / information practice and provision in a professional environment. *In* Brockman, Jr. pp.127-135.

9. Greenwood, J. Setting standards for quality assurance: the Canadian experience. *In* Taylor, M. H. and Wilson, T., eds. *Quality assurance in libraries: the health care sector.* Ottawa: Canadian Library Association; London: Library Association; London: Library Association Publishing, 1990, pp. 17-32.

10. Dawson, A. Quality first! The Taywood Information Centre and BS5750. *Aslib Information,* 1992, 20 (3) pp.112-113.

11. Shoolbred, M. BS 5750 and total quality management. *State Librarian.* (In the press)

12. Wales, J. L. Information Services Manager, ICI Chemicals and Polymers Ltd., Cheshire. (Personal communication)

13. Walton, M. *Deming management at work.* London: Mercury, 1990, pp.49-50, 71-73.

14. Williams, K. H. Manager, Wyerhauser Corporate Libraries, Washington. (Personal communication)

15. Cottrell, J. Favourable recipe. *TQM Magazine* 4 (1) February 1992, pp.17-20.

16. Florida Power & Light reins in its pioneering quality program. *The Raglan Report* 21 (47) April 21, 1991, pp.1-2.

17. Crosby, P. *Let's talk quality*. New York: McGraw-Hill, 1989. [Audio cassettes]

18. Civil Service College. *Prospectus 1992 to 1993*. Sunningdale, 1992, pp.15, 147.

19. Vickers, B. A fighting chance. *The TQM Magazine* 2 October 1990, pp.271-273.

20. Total quality management topic of SLA seminar. *Library Hotline* February 2, 1992, p.4.

Strategic Quality Management in Libraries

Donald E. Riggs

University Library, University of Michigan, Ann Arbor, Michigan 48109

I. Introduction

Strategic planning became an important management process in the corporate world during the 1960s. This type of planning is not something that is separate and distinct from the process of management; strategic planning is inextricably interwoven into the entire fabric of management. Not-for-profit organizations and service institutions began adopting strategic planning during the 1980s. It has proved to be the best type of planning available because it touches every aspect of the institution/organization. Several libraries and the American Library Association (ALA) have become very involved with strategic planning.

In the 1980s, a new way of looking at the management of corporations surfaced in the United States. Total quality management (TQM), having been used by the Japanese since the 1950s, began catching the attention of American businesses. W. Edwards Deming tried to get the U.S. businesses to use TQM in the 1950s, but was ignored in his own country. He was welcomed in Japan and became instrumental in turning the Japanese industry into an economic world power that still has many U.S. organizations reeling. The Japanese embraced Deming's program for managing productivity and quality, which gave them a 30-year head start on the United States. Strategic planning and TQM share many of the same management principles. They both emphasize forward thinking, teamwork, the human dimension, a culture change, enhanced productivity, and strategies for improving quality. In a sense, they go together like hand-in-glove. It would be counterproductive for a library to implement TQM without already having a planning process in place, and if this planning activity is to be effective, it must include the components of strategic planning.

II. Preliminary Steps

A. Strategic Vision

Libraries are undergoing one of the most difficult times in their history. For example, services are expanding while the size of the library staff is remaining stable or decreasing. Greater productivity is expected with fewer resources. The gigantic increase in new information and knowledge resources places greater stress on the staff and compounds the situation of "doing more with less." In recent years, more prognosticators are predicting the demise of libraries as they are currently configurated.

Library managers are positioned to take the leadership in creating the future of libraries. Their strategic vision is crucial if libraries are to be better understood and treated more favorably by funding sources. The strategic vision sets forth the direction the library will be going in the next decade. It is written in an abstract manner; however, the strategic vision's simulation of the future will likely be on target. The vision will include the library's potential for following various alternative courses. Although identification of the "right" course of action is far more significant than generating numbers of alternatives, the fact that more alternatives are brought forth for review may produce ideas that a lesser effort would not (Steiner, 1979). The successful implementation of the principles of TQM will depend, to a large extent, on how carefully crafted the vision statement is.

B. Mission

The library's mission statement is based on the vision statement. And the mission statement is also written in the abstract; it does, however, address the current as well as the future state of the library. A stated mission should never be considered "carved in stone." It should encourage creative growth via strategic planning and TQM, and the mission statement should also give the library legitimacy in the construct of its parent institution. The importance of the library's mission statement is not to be discounted, since all goals, objectives, strategies, and policies are predetermined by the organization's mission. Following is an example of a mission statement the author (Riggs, 1982, p. 2) coordinated the creation of:

> The primary responsibility of the Arizona State University Libraries is the support of the current and anticipated instructional, research, and service programs of the University. The responsibility entails the procurement, organization, preservation, and availability of library resources necessary for these programs.

C. Goals

Goals follow the mission statement in the strategic plan. They are broad general statements or desired or intended accomplishments. Goals are normally long-term in nature (e.g., 2 to 5 years). Goals play a prominent role in the implementation of TQM; the writing of the library goals should evolve from the team work that is advocated by TQM. Goals should never be written in isolation or by one person, nor should they extend beyond the realm of reality. Moreover, goals must be capable of being converted into specific, measurable objectives.

D. Objectives

Objectives begin to bring more focus to the library's intentions. They are stated in more specific terms than goals, and they are more internally focused. They are purposeful, short-term, consistent with goals, linked to other objectives, precise, measurable, and understandable.

While formulating objectives for a nonprofit organization such as a library, Hardy (1972, p. 65) recommends that the following questions be asked:

1. Is the objective designed to contribute directly to the achievement of one or more goals?

2. Is the objective feasible in the light of internal/external constraints?

3. Is the objective measurable? Are the results observable?

4. Were those who are accountable for achievement involved in setting the objectives?

5. Does the objective have a challenging quality?

After all objectives are written for the respective goals, they should be place in priority order. The ranking of the objectives should be based on reality. Are they achievable within the designated time period? The success of strategic planning and TQM depends on realistic projections, not on fantasies and unachievable dreams.

III. Strategies

After the vision statement, mission, goals, and objectives of the library have been established, the next step is to formulate program strategies. Through strategies, all goals and objectives of strategic planning and TQM will be realized. There is no more important part in the strategic planning/TQM process than actually dealing with strategies (Riggs, 1984). And one must not forget that strategies directly involve the human dimension in their formulation and implementation. Strategies are the specific major courses of actions or patterns of action for achieving goals and objectives. They are normally well conceived and well planned, but they can emerge from ad hoc situations. A strategy entails an explanation of what means will be used to achieve goals/objectives. There are many types of strategies; they include

1. Organizational strategies

2. Personnel strategies

3. Growth strategies

4. Opportunistic strategies

5. Innovation strategies

6. Financial strategies

7. Retrenchment strategies

Strategies will vary according to the circumstances. Their effectiveness depends on how well they are linked to the goals and objectives. After each year, and sometimes during the course of the year, the strategies have to be assessed to see if they are getting expected results. It is not uncommon to merge strategies, create substrategies, and even dissolve some of them. The author (Riggs, 1984, pp. 46-47) has determined that the effectiveness of strategies can be gauged by the following six criteria:

1. Internal consistency

2. Consistency with external environment

3. Appropriateness in view of resources

4. Acceptable degree of risk

5. Appropriate timetable

6. Workability

IV. The Next Moves: Implementing TQM Principles

A. Focus on Quality

After the strategic plan is in place, the principles of TQM are to be given high emphasis. Quality is the alpha and omega of TQM. Quality improvement becomes a way of life in the library. Coupling the principles of strategic planning with those of TQM creates a powerful management tool for the library. Strategic quality management coalesces new and old ideas; greater attention is given to systematic thinking, statistical process control, theories of human behavior, and transformational leadership. All of these emphases come together to form a new culture for the library.

Three prominent gurus of TQM have been recognized throughout management literature. They are Philip Crosby, W. Edwards Deming, and Joseph Juran. Juran followed Deming to Japan and also worked with Japanese industries on the improvement of quality. He first coined the term "fitness for use or purpose" and distinguished if from the definition of quality often used, "conformance to specifications." In Juran's view, less than 20 percent of quality problems are due to workers, with the remainder caused by management (compared with Deming's 94 percent). Juran is adamant that top management needs to be involved in TQM because he believes that all major quality problems are interdepartmental. Juran's 10 steps to quality improvement (Oakland, 1989, p. 289) are

1. Build awareness of the need and opportunity for improvement

2. Set goals for improvement

3. Organize to reach the goals (e.g., establish a quality council, design team, teams with the library, designate trainers)

4. Provide training

5. Carry out projects to solve problems

6. Report progress

7. Give recognition

8. Communicate results

9. Keep score

10. Maintain momentum by making annual improvement part of the organization's regular systems and processes

Crosby is best known for the concept of "zero defects" that he developed during the early 1960s while in charge of quality for different missile projects. Like the other TQM gurus, Crosby is a strong believer that top management has to have a visible commitment to quality. He observes that committed management can obtain a 40 percent reduction in error rates very quickly from a committed workforce. Crosby believes that many companies compound quality problems by "hassling" their employees and demotivating them by using "thoughtless, irritating, unconcerned" ways of dealing with people (Oakland, 1989, p. 282). The main strength of Crosby's program is the attention it gives to transforming quality culture. His program involves everyone in the organization by stressing individual conformance to requirements. Because of his focus on first changing the management culture. Crosby's approach is clearly a top-down process. He is best known for defining the new management culture with his four "absolutes" of quality management (Lowe and Mazzeo, 1986, p. 24):

1. Definition of quality: Conformance to requirements

2. System: Prevention

3. Performance standard: Zero defects

4. Measurement: Cost of quality

The above "absolutes" are self-explanatory and they give management a very explicit plan for managing the transition to quality improvement.

W. Edwards Deming is often referred to as the "father" of TQM. He earned this recognition by being one of the very first people to preach the attributes of TQM. When he visits American businesses, he excoriates them for their cheap, shoddy goods; he tells them that an emphasis on quality will reap lasting benefits in market share and profitability; and he lays out principles for making quality a strategic advantage. This article, or any serious piece on TQM, would be remiss without delineating Deming's 14 points for management to follow in quality improvement. Entire books (e.g., Miller, 1991) have been written with their focus on Deming's 14 points.

1. Maintain consistency of purpose for the improvement of product and service.

2. Adopt the new philosophy of refusing to allow defects.

3. Cease the dependence on mass inspection and rely only on statistical control.

4. End the practice of awarding business on price tag alone (provide statistical evidence of quality).

5. Improve the system of production and service.

6. Institute training.

7. Institute leadership, giving all employees the proper tools to do the job right.

8. Drive out fear; encourage communication and productivity.

9. Encourage different departments to work together on problem solving.

10. Eliminate posters and slogans that do not teach specific improvement methods.

11. Use statistical methods to continuously improve quality and productivity; eliminate numerical quotas.

12. Eliminate all barriers to pride in workmanship.

13. Provide ongoing training to keep apace with changing products, methods, services, etc.; institute a vigorous program of education and retraining.

14. Clearly define top management's permanent commitment to quality; take action to accomplish the transformation.

From the foregoing descriptions of the gurus' philosophies on quality improvement, one can readily extract their difference in some concepts. For example, one of Crosby's slogans calls for zero deficits in a product, whereas Deming's 10th point is to "eliminate slogans, exhortations, and targets for work force." Deming's 8th point warns managers to "drive out fear" so that employees can do their jobs, while Juran believes, "fear can bring out the best in people."

The differences among Crosby, Deming, and Juran are small when compared with their many similarities. Each of these three gurus, along with most other authorities in TQM, agrees that to have a TQM program an organization has to

1. Have a "total" commitment to quality

2. Be customer (user) driven

3. Eliminate rework

4. Place emphasis on teamwork

5. Give high priority to training

6. Show respect for all people in the organization, and empower people throughout the organization

7. Create an ongoing appreciation for quality

The remainder of this article will focus on the above seven areas and their application in libraries.

B. Total Commitment

The world "total" in TQM has special significance. If the library intends to implement TQM, it most certainly should not plan on doing so without total commitment. The library director must be fully committed to making the principles of TQM work. And this commitment has to be evident throughout the library. Ideally, the library's parent institution will be engaged in TQM. Deming believes that having a firm commitment from the top is the most important step in implementing TQM (Petersen and Hillkirk, 1991). Failure on the part of top management to be deeply involved with strategic planning and TQM will give good cause for other library staff members not to be fully committed. Resources will have to allocate to the strategic quality management (SQM) program. All services and products provided by the library should come under the scrutiny of TQM. The coupling of strategic planning and TQM serves as a safety measure in assuring that the entire library will be involved in SQM. The system, rather than the employee, should come under the microscope. All of the work procedures/processes in the library should be studied to seek out problems that prevent quality. A common language should prevail throughout the library about SQM. Enthusiasm and accountability are good features to display early in the implementation stage. Early success stories will help to make believers and encourage other successful endeavors. Peters and Austin (1985) believe that quality is a hands-on proposition.

The total commitment to SQM has to be reflected in the library's vision statement, mission, goals, and objectives. Strategies will also reenforce the commitment. Effective communication of the philosophy, expectations, and benefits of SQM is a must. The library director has to take the initiative in preparing the first few documents on the SQM; these communiques should be delivered to the entire library staff and its advisory boards/councils.

C. Customer (User) Driven Service

The proponents of TQM believe that the quality of an organization is determined by the customer/user satisfaction level. When one thinks of the satisfaction of library users, it becomes quite clear that libraries are natural beneficiaries of TQM. Libraries are one of society's best service organizations. Librarians have exercised a strong service philosophy for the past century or more. Nevertheless, there is always room for improvement in the quality of services. After many years of providing excellent service to users, librarians have fallen short in their understanding of how their patrons actually learn. Library schools have been remiss in not focusing a course or two on the theories of learning. Librarians should have a better grasp of, for example, the theory of cognitive learning. The recent arrival of the online public access catalog has reaffirmed the need for a better understanding of the patron's learning patterns. Interaction between the human and the machine is a complex endeavor and one that requires more research. Library users normally have a more sophisticated understanding of computers than librarians believe. Also, their expectations are higher than may be anticipated. For example, users are beginning to ask questions such as, "Why does the library have so many terminals to access various databases?" "Why does one have to use an OCLC terminal to access the OCLC database, why not have one terminal that will access all databases?" "Why aren't the CD-ROM databases in the online public access catalog?" These are all good, logical questions; the users deserve to know that the local library does not have control over which terminals can access the various databases, if that is indeed the case.

Libraries exist for the people for whom they serve, and not for the people who work in them. This truism carries much meaning. However, sometimes the library staff tends to forget the reason for the library's existence. The people who work in the library are the library's most important resource. And the services delivered to the users will come essentially from the work of the library staff. SQM places a high premium on both the users and the library staff.

As part of the strategic planning process, the library should conduct an environmental scan. This study should include a survey of the users' satisfaction level. To make the study more objective, the library should employ an independent person or firm to conduct the survey. The library would work with the person/firm in establishing areas that should be surveyed [e.g., collections, reference assistance, help screens on OPACs (online public assistance catalogs)]; after the areas have been identified, the library would cease its involvement in the study. Space should be available on the survey form that would encourage the user to list areas where the library could be more helpful, recommendations for improving service (e.g., establishing a telephone renewal service for checked-out books), and some of the things that the library does that the patron does not find useful.

SQM will provide a new mind-set regarding the user. Some long-held assumptions will be challenged. Services will be examined more carefully and analyzed in a quantitative manner (Coffey, Eisenberg, Gaucher, and Kratochwill, 1991). Pilot projects will be necessary before long-term commitments are made to full-fledged endeavors.

D. Eliminate Rework

One of the obvious principles of SQM is that of doing one's job better and providing the user a value-added quality product/service. The library staff members should understand that their work is in direct relation to the user's needs. Questions like "Are we doing the right things for our users?" and "If not, how can we improve our work processes?" should be occasionally posed.

It is human nature to continue doing things the way they have always been done without pausing to ask, "Why am I doing this work, and who will it benefit?" Libraries have made some signal improvements in work processes in recent years. Some of these improvements have resulted from the use of technology. A few years ago, libraries would direct the staff to write specific information (e.g., vendor price) on the verso of the title page and stamp the "secret" page. Such work has been eliminated in many libraries.

Because much of library work is task oriented and labor intensive, all levels of library employees eventually do some of all types of work; therefore, it is easy for the professional staff to get bogged down in the mundane tasks that can be performed by others. Due to staffing shortages, some of this type of work may not be avoided in the smaller libraries. Nevertheless, it is almost criminal for professional staff to fulfill their day's work doing these mundane tasks. They must be involved with the more intellectually demanding work, be creative in offering more refined services for users, and take the initiative in solving workflow problems.

SQM stresses that the library should simplify, standardize, and get the work done right the first time. The time spent fixing earlier mistakes, in useless work that has to be redone, and in extra steps that add little or no value to the product or service result in a huge amount of unproductive time and generally bring little benefit to the library user. One of the first steps necessary in improving workflow is to conduct a work sampling. Various types of sampling techniques are available to assist in detecting errors in current work activities (Fuller, 1985).

E. Teamwork

Little or no progress will be made in implementing the principles of SQM without teamwork. From the library director's office to the mail room, within departments and among them, quality issues are attacked in teams. One should not confuse teams with the typical library committees. Teams are better characterized as "self-directed work groups." Teams bring together most or all library staff who work in an area to improve the respective area's quality. All persons on the SQM team will share responsibility and will benefit from "team learning." Developing a strategic plan for reference service is an example where the team approach will function well. Teams can comprise either persons from a respective department/unit or there can be cross-departmental teams.

The focus of SQM can be on many dimensions of the library. For example, a team could zero in on how to improve a particular library service area by studying how to improve the way the work gets done (the methods) rather than simply assessing what is done (the results). Scholtes in his *The Team Handbook* (1988, pp. 5-68) states that

> The main difference between projects under previous styles of management and those run under quality improvement is summed up in one word: planning. Teams must spend time in the early stages of their projects planning how the project will unfold. Planning is the heart of using a scientific approach to quality improvement. Only then can teams study the correct problems, gather data that will prove useful, and learn from experience.

F. Training

Implementation of SQM in libraries cannot be done without additional costs. Wide-range training is essential. Leadership training, library-wide training, specific program training, and department/unit level training are some examples of necessary human resource investments to get the SQM process off the ground. If library leaders think they can implement the principles of strategic planning and TQM without any additional costs, then they should get their heads out of the sand. Without the training sessions, SQM will be a colossal failure. The right hand must know what the left hand is doing.

When the trainers are being trained, they will glean a better understanding about the importance of improving service for the user — this thrust will be the cornerstone for all SQM activities. One of the goals for the training program should be that of developing the skills and abilities of the library staff so that they will ultimately be able to bring about improvement in users' services. Furthermore, the training program should encourage creativity and innovative potential of each library employee.

Proper training will provide the cadre of library staff to teach others how to implement SQM in their respective areas. Teaching the proper use of SQM tools and techniques will repay the library huge dividends. Excellence in library services is a constantly moving target. Training can create the framework and structure to help guide the library toward the pursuit of quality improvement.

G. Empowering and Respecting People

One of the many attributes of SQM is the change of culture within the library. Decisions will be pushed down to the lowest level. Many of today's large libraries continue to function as bureaucracies. Most decisions come up to and are made in the director's office. Staff members in these bureaucratic libraries are treated with little respect.

Most of the gurus of TQM believe that most of an organization's problems are traceable to the process itself and few problems can be attributed to the staff. They advocate that administrators should stop attacking people and look more critically at the processes/systems. TQM is known for empowering people. People generally want to do the right thing and they want pride in their work. Whenever surveys are conducted on why librarians chose librarianship as their profession, most of the respondents indicate that they went into the field because they like providing service to others and they enjoy working with information and knowledge resources. With a strong desire to provide service to others, librarians are already geared for SQM. Now what they need is the "empowerment" to do their work as effectively as possible. Library managers bear the responsibility of removing barriers that prevent their staff from functioning fully. Giving the people who actually do the work (those who are closest to the processes) empowerment to change things that are obviously done wrong and deter service for users is a wise step in the SQM direction.

Many of the morale problems in libraries are created and perpetuated by library managers. They may lack good people skills, be poor communicators, or simply not understand basic principles of humanistic management. SQM, through team work, training, and empowerment, will raise the respect for all of the employees in the library. Invisible walls between the professional and nonprofessional staff will disappear when the library has developed teams to work on strategies for achieving goals and objectives. Self-respect will also be garnered when the empowerment of the staff allows full contribution and satisfaction.

Empowering the library staff and showing necessary respect for them will be one of the best things achieved in any library. Most of the actual work in libraries is done by the rank and file. This valuable group of employees is at the "moment of truth" everyday in dealing with the users. It only follows logic that if they are treated well, empowered, and respected, the library will be a much better place for the user.

H. Ongoing Process

SQM is not a one-time deal. It should not be set in place only in bad financial times. And it should not be purported as a panacea for all library problems. In a sense, it should not be described as a "change of things," but as a "way of life." Continuous improvement in the library's services and products is the chief rationale for using SQM.

Unlike traditional planning, strategic planning is an ongoing planning process. SQM, like its strategic planning component, should be recognized as a management process that is going to be part of the library for a long, long time.

V. Conclusion

Inventing the future and strategic directions for the library and making them happen are awesome responsibilities. Library managers need as much help as possible with this endeavor. Combining the principles of strategic planning and TQM is an approach that is difficult to quibble with when one considers the various management processes. SQM will produce many refined, value-added services/products for library users. The total library staff will be more productive and will significantly enjoy their work more. Work will be simplified and streamlined; some procedures/processes will be eliminated. There will be many frustrations associated with implementing SQM. Some staff will initially resist it; some will wonder why the library is asking the already overstressed staff to take on this additional responsibility. Training will be expensive and it will evolve slower than one desires. Teams will express dissatisfaction about the amount of time it takes to bring about "a new way of doing things." And there will be some disagreements about the new way(s) things should be done (Chaffee, 1990).

In a nutshell, despite various frustrations, SQM, when fully implemented, will result in a significant improvement for library users. Tangible enhancements will be evident in workflow throughout the library. One of the more important benefits to the library will be the culture change that SQM has created in how the library staff has become involved in assessing the various operations, participating in determining strategic directions for the library, and functioning as a team. Strategic quality improvement is a phenomenon that offers an opportunity to dramatically transform some areas of the library, implement quality-driven programs, focus more on the users, and provide the library with a healthy "gust of fresh air."

> Opportunity rarely knocks on your door,
> Knock rather on opportunity's door if you ardently wish to enter.
> B. C. Forbes

References

Chaffee, E. E. (1990). Quality: Key to the future. *American Journal of Pharmaceutical Education* 54, 349-352.

Coffey, R. J., Eisenberg, M., Gaucher, E. M., and Kratochwill, E. W. (1991). Total quality progress at the University of Michigan Medical Center. *Journal of Quality and Production* 17, 22-33.

Fuller, F. T. (1985). Eliminating complexity from work: Improving productivity by enchancing quality. *National Productivity Review* 4, 337-344.

Hardy, J. M. (1972). *Corporate Planning for Nonprofit Organizations.* Associated Press, New York.

Lowe, T. A., and Mazzeo, J. M. (1986). Three preachers, one religion. *Quality* 9, 22-25.

Miller, R. I. (1991). *Applying the Deming Method to Higher Education.* College and University Personnel Association, Washington, D.C.

Oakland, J. S. (1989). *Total Quality Management.* Heinemann Professional Publishing, Ltd., Oxford.

Peters, T., and Austin, N. (1985). *A Passion for Excellence: The Leadership Difference.* Random House, New York.

Petersen, D. E., and Hillkirk, J. (1991). *A Better Idea: Redefining the Way Americans Work.* Houghton Mifflin, Boston.

Riggs, D. E. (1982). *Arizona State University Libraries' Annual Report.* Arizona State University, Tempe.

Riggs, D. E. (1984). *Strategic Planning for Library Managers.* Oryx Press, Phoenix.

Scholtes, P. R. (1988). *The Team Handbook.* Joiner Associates, Inc., Madison, Wisconsin.

Steiner, G. A. (1979). *Strategic Planning: What Every Manager Must Know.* Free Press, New York.

Quality in Library and Information Service: A Review

Tom Whitehall

Tom Whitehall is a Lecturer at the Department of Information and Library Studies, Loughborough University, UK.

Quality is not a new word in the library and information world. In 1969, Lancaster[1] suggested that the criteria he found to be important to the success of searches in the *Index Medicus* database could be of use for quality control of the database. Now we have "quality circles" and "total quality management", but these seem to be more about participative problem solving than the sort of systematic search after quality with which Lancaster was concerned.

The current interest in "quality assurance" has apparently arisen from a need to ensure that a quality control system is in place to offset "value for money", in cases when this means producing services more cheaply. This is because crude output measures such as issue figures and membership statistics are irrelevant in showing the extent to which services have become less individual and more formal, as a result of reduced funding. Also quality becomes very important when we try for increased return on investment in services by attempting to increase their use.

Writers on quality tend to complain that there is no theoretical basis for understanding and using the concept in management. In fact, quality has been thought about and written about most usefully over the years, but not necessarily under that name. The main purpose of this review is to bring together present concerns and past work on the quality of library and information services. The review is about the quality of a *service*, not just the quality of information.

What Is Quality and What Is It For?

If quality did not exist, it would have to be invented to satisfy a need. When you have decided what you are going to do for clients, and how you are going to do it, there may be a feeling that what is being done could be done better for them. This feeling is about quality. Orr[2] defined quality as "how good is the service?", and refused to go further, on the grounds

(From *Library Management,* Vol. 13, No. 5. Copyright 1992. Reprinted with permission of MCB University Press.)

that an intuitive definition was more useful. W. B. Rouse[3] compared quality of service with the "adequacy" of a table or chair for its purpose in life. This suggests a minimum standard of suitability, which could be achieved by the optimization of a few basic criteria which have to do with the functions of a table or chair. So quality is *something felt* by the users of a service, but it is also a *property* of the service itself. Wilson[4] makes an analogy with a retail store, where quality is recognized by the client in terms of ease of movement, clear signposting, up-to-date stock, and approachable, knowledgeable staff.

From both analogies we can see how useful it is to be able to improve the quality of a service. For example, if you are going to charge for a service, or are in competition with others to provide it, then the shining quality of your service will help to sell it to the clients. Quality is a useful bargaining counter in negotiation with the funder. (If it can be shown that a service falls below accepted quality standards in some particular, a request for money to restore it may be granted.) In the choice between alternative approaches to, say, current awareness service or reference retrieval, quality is as important as cost. A demonstration of "the supplier's capability to control the processes which determine the acceptability of the product supplied"[5] is a useful safeguard in contracting out services. A quality survey may be required as part of self-evaluation of a service prior to its accreditation.[6]

What Is Quality About, And How Can It Be Appraised?

The relationship of quality to the other concerns of service managers is not at all straightforward. It is said that cost efficiency is about processes internal to a service organization, whereas quality is about the impact of the client.[7] This is certainly true about the place in which each is noticed. Strictly speaking, cost-efficiency is about the cost of obtaining unit outputs, like a book ready to put on the shelf or a reference from a database. On the other hand, quality is about criteria more relevant to the client's reaction to the service, like the coverage of a library collection, or the response time of an online search; but these are criteria of process as well! Perhaps this is why cost-efficiency and quality enjoy a close relationship as rivals. If the production of services is systematically made cheaper, then their quality may suffer.

For appraisal purposes it is helpful to distinguish quality from value. It is commonly said nowadays that quality is connected with the outcome of a service. This must be so, because it is the user who senses quality. However, *value* is also connected with outcome. We can see this best in terms of the client as a *doppelgänger*. A person approaches the service and tries to use it. The immediate outcome is one of ease of use or, alternatively, of frustration. This user feels the *quality* of the service. The user as a worker or liver may gain something from the act of use, as a result of some piece of information or a document retrieved, or simply because the service was performed for him or her. This user feels the service's *value*.

How can the quality of a service be discovered from its outcome? Not—as has been suggested in the context of a quality assurance programme for a health enquiry service—but knowing whether there were any improvements in the enquirer's circumstances as a result of receiving the information, since this is about value, not quality.[8] To think of measuring the improvement in a student's ability to write essays as a test of the quality of an interlibrary loan service[9] is pointless for the same reason. If it could be undertaken, however, it would be a useful measure of the service's value to the student.

Self-Evaluation

Can library and information workers assess quality by themselves, as participants in, and planners of, services? This is obviously the most convenient way to do it. However, for such assessments to be credible, the assessors would need to have an agreed analysis of what was quality, and how it was to be assessed—something which still has to be provided. In peer review,[10] for example, we have a promising *method* for self-evaluation, but we need user-derived criteria, and standards for these criteria, to make it work for us.

User Satisfaction With a Service

Librarians have tried to appraise quality by asking users whether they were satisfied with an act of use. However, clients are known to express satisfaction in spite of how they really feel.[11, 12, 13] These generous expressions of satisfaction ("It wasn't their fault they couldn't find it")[14] are unlikely to be of use for justification purposes. They are certainly not useful in improving the quality of service. Even if a rating on a scale of satisfaction is obtained,[15] which tells us that the clients do not like the service as it stands, all we can do about it is to sleep fitfully at night. Without further investigation we know that something is wrong, but not what is wrong.

Success in determining quality from consumer opinion has come from asking *the right questions* of people who are *known to have used* a service. In a user satisfaction survey, an invitation to be critical works well, and successful quality evaluations of this type have concentrated on one service at a time (in the sense of enquiry service, document delivery service, reference retrieval service, and so on). Stradling[16] asked for "comments, criticisms or suggestions" on each separate service, rather than on his library as a whole, and obtained some useful information about his loan service and bookstock, readers' advisory service, the catalogue, and the reference library.

Pryor[17] asked his users to mention the best and worst features of the information services at NASA. It is interesting that he had interviewed only 16 of his 1,000 clients when a consistent picture emerged of what was wrong with the reference retrieval service (the response time was too slow, the abstracts were not detailed enough, and the indexing had not kept up with current ideas in the area.) To determine the *value* of a service, it is necessary to ask all its users and take the sum of their replies, whereas it seems that problems of *quality* can be discovered with far less effort. Whitehall[18] used the "best and worst features" question to evaluate the quality of an information bulletin for academic staff at Trent Polytechnic, but also prompted clients from a checklist of quality criteria (coverage, timeliness, relevance, type and content of items chosen, format and arrangement of the bulletin, and reading load for the client).

Encouraging clients to take a fresh look at a service seems to be a useful approach to finding evidence for improving its quality. Slater[19] asked clients what sort of service they *wanted* and received replies (easy to use, proactive, customized to the individual's specific requirements) which could be taken as comments on the quality of the service they were *receiving*. Similarly, Kaske and Sanders,[20] in a series of group interviews with librarians and clients, asked "What would you like the catalogue to do which it does not do now?", which yielded such replies as give access to the book's index, table of contents, and foreword).

Not everyone is happy with accepting evidence about the quality of a service from its user, however.

First, writers on evaluation make much of the subjective nature of user evaluation, as if this were a problem. However, is it not true to say that a value attributed to information supplied can be *only* subjective (since it depends on the use of the information by an individual or team)? Over the years, surveys have identified again and again the common problems which users have with the quality of services. Does this not mean that suspicion about the "subjectivity" of these judgements has to give way to acceptance of the series of useful quality criteria which has emerged?

Second, it has often been suggested that users may not be competent to judge the effectiveness of services. From one point of view this is nonsense, because it is the users who *feel* quality. When it comes to quality, they are the experts. On the other hand, the view that users are unable to judge does make some sense, because users can have different ideas about the relative importance of criteria critical to quality, according to their need (for example, differing emphasis on novelty and precision ratios, as measure of the success of reference retrieval[21]). User ideas about a numerical optimum for criteria will differ for the same reason (for example, different ideas about waiting time for an interlibrary loan or currency of a current awareness notification). In a survey of users' reactions to a service they may need to be prompted about specific criteria because the average person does not subject a service to rigorous analysis—he/she uses it and is thankful.

Failure Analysis

A source of information on quality which is significantly different from asking for user opinion is observation or simulation of an act of use. If things go wrong, an attempt is made to find out why. In the attempt, shortcomings of the service may be revealed. The coverage of library collections, the availability of books on the shelves, the adequacy of catalogues, and the accuracy of answers to enquiries, are among aspects of library quality which have been examined in this way.

For example, Line[22] and Lewis[23] asked academic staff to note down references they came across and thought they might like to consult. Then they looked to see what percentage of these were in their libraries.

Quigley[24] reported a failure analysis investigation aimed at improving cataloguing and book selection. Requests received at branch libraries were looked up in the catalogue and, if it was difficult to satisfy them, an analysis was made of the reasons. Lipetz[25] stopped users with "What were you about to do here at the catalogue when I interrupted you?", and enquired about what information they had brought with them. After their search, users were asked if it had been successful. If not, the reasons were found by investigation at the catalogue. Markey[26] used a tape recorder to note down the spoken thoughts of people as they searched the catalogue. If they were quiet, they were prompted to speak! The interviewer also made notes on the searcher's behaviour.

Failure analysis and user satisfaction surveys are time-consuming and costly. Perhaps we do not need to use them as a regular part of quality appraisal. Because the same problems have been uncovered again and again, over the years, we could in many areas simply test for the problems.

Performance Measures

It would be convenient if published performance measures could be used for testing the quality of library and information service. To some extent, this is possible. However, most measures do not give adequately detailed information about what is wrong with a service to enable corrective action to be planned.

Several measures are available to assess how much a service is used by the client community for which it is intended (its so-called "penetration"), for example: number of enquiries per head of population served; average annual loans per capita; in-library materials use per capita.[27] However, penetration of the client community is not a *diagnostic* measure of service quality. There are several different reasons why penetration could be low. The service could be irrelevant, or difficult to use, or not very accessible, or just not known about or understood. Thus, having made a survey and obtained a low penetration ratio, one is left with a question: What *is* wrong with the service?

Performance measures which have been proposed to measure satisfied demand could be used to make inferences about the quality of a service—for example, user satisfaction with a recent use, on a scale;[28, 29] or the proportion of satisfied searches for material by author, by title, by subject, during a user's visit.[27] However, low measurements for consumer satisfaction can tell us that something is wrong with a service, but not *what* is wrong. For example, poor satisfaction of known item or subject searches could be explained by problems with finding aids, or collection coverage, or the availability of material owned. All these possibilities would have to be investigated before any action could be taken.

Some performance measures provide information on quality directly, without further enquiry being necessary, because they are concerned with individual quality criteria. Some examples of these useful measures are given below, listed under specific criteria:

(1) *Measures of accessibility*: proportion of the target population who live or work more than a certain distance from the library;[30] availability of books owned;[28] time at which professional staff are available at the desk.[28]

(2) *Measures of response time*: percentage of requests for information filled on the same day;[27, 31] percentage of database searches done on the day of request, and on the following day;[32] percentage of interlibrary loan requests filled after two weeks, after three weeks.[32]

(3) *Measures of collection coverage*: percentage of journals and monographs cited by faculty in targeted subject areas which are in the library collection;[32] fraction of books in the field which the library has acquired.[31]

(4) *Measures of relevance of stock*: average annual use per item of stock (the so-called "turnover rate").[27, 29]

These performance measures can be used directly in a quality control scheme, if standards are set for optimization of the criteria they cover. But from where will these standards come?

Standards of Quality

As Martin suggests, "Most standards in the library field have not been designed as aids in evaluation".[33] Standards for inputs do not guarantee quality of service,[34] although they could well be preconditions of effectiveness.[13] Standards should be based on research into effectiveness, not on conjecture or subjective opinion.[35] For instance, Bunge[36] showed the relevance of training to the speed of dealing with an enquiry, which suggests the rather obvious standard that people giving an enquiry service should be trained in the use of relevant sources, and in question negotiation, before being let loose on the public.

For critical aspects of service which can be expressed numerically the question arises, should standards be minimal, average, or optimal/ideal? Local standards can be optimal, representing the best possible performance within local constraints. A *range* of acceptable performance is another possibility, or a minimal standard can be set, and then raised, if individual performance is consistently better than the standard. As Stodulski says, "Standards allow us to compete with ourselves".[37]

At least one writer on quality appraisal sees standards as a direct challenge to staff and suppliers: "equipment in the Health Sciences Library will require no servicing", "staff members will have no lost time in accidents", "all cataloguing will be done consistently". However, McFarlane[38] does allow that records of non-compliance are collected, and periodic tests are made.

A useful approach to evaluation using a standard is suggested by Bourne[39] in the idea of "the 90 percent library". This library satisfies its users 90 percent of the time (any other suitable figure can be used). So 90 percent of the information needs of its users are satisfied by document provision in less than n days, searches made in less than n days, enquiries answered in less than n days, a current awareness service which furnishes information from primary material not less than n days old, with a processing time of less than n days, and so on. Mary Cronin[32] has suggested standards of this sort for interlibrary loans, collection coverage, and reference retrieval services.

Devising a Quality Assurance Scheme

It is interesting to see the different ways in which recent writers have approached the analysis of the quality assurance (QA) problem.

Quality control by imposing the QA scheme of the organization to which one belongs is not recommended.[40] A medical library in a hospital, for example, is one level removed from patient care and would find clinical output measures irrelevant.

At the heart of most schemes is the setting of standards, and a monitoring process to check the extent to which these are being maintained. The standards are numeric targets, or qualitative guidelines at the level of a single aspect or process associated with a specific service—for example, as part of the document supply service "to supply interlibrary loans three weeks from the request",[9] as part of collection development "to provide 75 percent of journals and 80 percent of monographs needed by faculty for research",[32] and for an information service to keep information sheets up to date and verify the accuracy of information annually, and not to attempt to give advice or counselling.[8] However, not all analyses have been taken to the level of individual services; for example, the NCC checklist[41] includes quite general criteria of quality, such as library location, opening hours and layout.

Monitoring is done by logging what happens over a test period, or by random sampling.[42] Measurement should ideally be plotted on to quality control charts with confidence limits marked.[43, 44]

Regarding the derivation of the targets and guidelines on which a scheme is based, there appear to be three different approaches: looking around for problems and attempting their resolution in terms of setting targets;[9, 45, 46] surveying or listening to user requirements and expectations, and making these the subject of standards;[8, 32, 41] using a top-down analysis of library work, from mission statement through main objectives and service objectives to the processes necessary to achieve them, and the targets needed to control the processes.[37, 47]

It has to be said that those who have tried the top-down approach seem not to have been satisfied with the results. A top-down analysis was seen as a valuable reference guide for use in decision making. However action on quality assurance had still to be thought out at a service level.

As well as formal objectives at the process level, based on quality targets and guidelines, several schemes include objectives to *improve on* present performance within a specified time: for example, to increase the average range of correct responses to enquiries from the present level to 80 percent within two years.[32]

However, most reported QA schemes do not seem to cover all the quality criteria for the service under review, but just those identified by problems which arose in a library, or those disclosed by comments made by clients as a result of a satisfaction survey, or which were revealed by a top-down analysis of the library's mission. A serious situation arises if problem spotting or top-down analysis on their own are used in drafting a quality scheme: such a scheme may miss altogether criteria relevant to client convenience in using a service. At the extreme, these approaches used alone could produce a quality scheme which is about cost-efficient production of outputs, rather than the production of effective outputs (e.g., Gillespie's scheme for "quality appraisal" of new books processing[48]).

On the other hand, to carry out a client survey on each occasion when a quality review is undertaken seems very wasteful. This is because the literature of evaluation contains much useful information about what things the users of services have found to be critical to their ease of use. Practitioners could use these criteria and guidelines in their schemes for quality review.[40, 49, 50]

An attempt is made below to list, service by service, what has been discovered over the years about the key issues for client satisfaction, and also the methods which have been reported for obtaining feedback on the extent to which quality has been achieved.

Quality Review of Enquiry Service

"Enquiry service" here means that a client approaches library or information staff with a question which requires them to look for an answer and possibly to supply documents as well. For the purposes of analysis, the search stops short of reference retrieval from printed abstracts or a database. The key issues for client satisfaction appear to be: the coverage of the reference collection; the relevance and quality of the answers supplied; the accuracy of the answers; the speed of response; and the accessibility and ease of use of the service.

Coverage of the Reference Collection

Shortcomings in coverage are indicated by an analysis of rejected questions,[51] a failure analysis which points to stock deficiencies, or the discovery that outside sources have to be used very frequently in some areas.

To optimize coverage, several lists of materials in appropriate subject areas can be used to find relevant materials of different types.[11, 51] Electronic sources can be used where they allow access to more current material. A record should be kept of what sources are used to help with decisions about retention and renewal of reference stock.[52] The date distribution of reference books in the collection can be listed to check its accuracy.[53]

Relevance and Quality of Answers

For general information on question-answering performance, the client's reaction to the material or answer provided can be obtained.[8] Peer review of novices using a checklist[10] and peer coaching[54] have also been used. The question-negotiation ability of staff can be tested by asking questions which need some clarification.[55] Staff's knowledge and use of sources can be checked by observational testing, with questions formulated from material known to be in stock.[56] Whether staff use more than one source in a search is a good indicator of ability. Failure analysis pointing to poor search technique is another source of feedback.

The quality of the service can be optimized by using enquiry staff with good communication and decision-making ability, formal library qualifications, current general knowledge,[57] and subject knowledge in the areas of interest to clients.[11, 58] Staff should be trained in question negotiation,[36] have a critical knowledge of sources available in their library, and know what is available from outside. They should also know how to use the sources.[11, 36, 58] The client should be asked if he/she needs material to take away[8] and told what sources have been consulted in the search.[58]

Accuracy of Answers

Reference performance can be tested unobtrusively, using questions which call for up-to-date information or are known to be difficult to answer accurately.[59, 60, 61] Cronin[32] suggests, as an objective, that 80-90 percent of answers should be correct.

Staff selected for reference work should be careful and accurate people. They need to be trained to use current sources known to be accurate.[56] Where an information unit hands out pre-prepared information sheets, these should be checked regularly for currency and accuracy.[8] Any transcripts and typed answers supplied to clients should be checked; also any photocopies supplied should be checked for completeness and clarity, and accurately collated before being handed to the client. The source reference should be added.[58]

Speed of Response

The time taken to deal with enquiries is best established by unobtrusive testing. Gann[8] suggests that all enquiries should be handled within 24 hours. Cronin[32] suggests the objective that 75 percent of enquiries should have some results by the next day. Staff should ask about the urgency of a request early on.[58]

Optimization of response time is achieved through staff's knowledge of sources, their training in use of sources,[62] and their innate problem-solving ability.

Accessibility and Ease of Use of Service

The attitude of enquiry staff can be observed during unobtrusive testing.[55, 56, 60, 61] Young[63] and Judkins[58] used peer review employing a checklist to check staff attitudes. The clients should be asked about ease of use of the service.[8]

Obviously, enough staff need to be made available at enquiry desks, but staff selection and training are also relevant here. Courtesy, involvement and approachability are desirable traits. Confidentiality for the enquirer must be ensured.[58] Lopez and Rubacher[64] found that clients' satisfaction correlated well with the results of tests on reference staff, using scales developed for counsellors and psychotherapists to measure their empathy, genuineness and concreteness.

Quality Review of Document Provision Service

This section is concerned with those incidents when the library is asked to provide a copy of a specific book, or other document, already known to the client. The document may or may not be in the library. The key issues for client satisfaction appear to be: the coverage of the library's collection; the adequacy of the finding aids; the availability of material owned by the library; and the adequacy of interlibrary loan arrangements.

Collection Coverage

Excessive reliance on interlibrary loans to satisfy requests indicates poor coverage. To optimize collection coverage it is necessary to become aware of clients' needs and interests. Stock should be compared with users' interest profiles, expressed as class numbers.[65] Material which has been cited, or considered relevant by clients, should be listed and its availability in the library checked.[22, 23, 66] Stock should be checked against more than one booklist in the area.[67, 68, 69] Users, or a subject librarian, should be asked to take a critical look at the shelves.[68] In the case of a history collection,[70] it should be ascertained whether it contains the source material for the important secondary accounts. All publishers in the relevant subject area should be identified. Librarians with subject knowledge should be used for book selection.

Adequacy of Finding Aids

Requests for items known to be in stock, but the location of which cannot be discovered, or which clients report as "not in the library", may indicate problems with the catalogue.[25] (Before such leads are followed up, it should be checked that the client has *looked* at the catalogue, and the possibility that the item is missing from the shelf should be considered.)

To the extent that libraries have retained control over the contents of their catalogue, a liberal attitude to "name" cataloguing, and an entry for *all* items in stock, will make it easier for clients to locate material through the catalogue.[25, 71] Clients should know about any conventions used in deciding the order of items in the author or title sequences of a print or microfiche catalogue, and the conventions should be consistently applied by cataloguers.[25] Printed catalogues should have separate sequences for name, title, and subject entries.[72] A rotated title index to a printed catalogue makes it easier for forgetful clients to find a known item by its title.[73]

Availability of Material

Reports from clients of material not available on the shelf should be examined.[74-77] The contents of shelves should be checked against shelf-list and loan records, and missing items investigated.[15, 28]

There should be a short loan period for material in high demand, or extra copies should be purchased.[34, 78, 79] Speedy binding, or no binding at all, should be considered as a way of increasing availability of serial material.[78] Lost materials which are nevertheless in demand should be repurchased if possible. Material returned from use should be reshelved speedily and accurately. The library should be opened at times convenient to the clients and if possible located in a place convenient to them.[41]

Adequacy of Interlibrary Loan Arrangements

Information should be collected on time of request, time of sending the request to an outside source, time of arrival of the material, and time of notifying the client of its availability.[9] It should be established that the client still needs the item on its arrival.[16] Material should be supplied three weeks from the request;[9] 50 percent of material requested should be supplied in two weeks and 85 percent within three weeks from the date of request.[32]

Where the library is dependent for material on certain topics, they should be listed and outside sources of material in these areas identified. Users should be informed about any delay in supplying material ordered from another source.[9]

Quality Review of Computerized Reference Retrieval

Here a client is looking for references to documents on a named topic, and will want either to search alone or to delegate a search. The database may be of material kept locally, in which case it contains references to monographs, reports, conference proceedings and so on. It may, at the other extreme, be a commercially available database of references mainly to articles in the periodical literature.

The key issues for client satisfaction appear to be: the coverage of the database by subject and type of material; accessibility and ease of use of the system itself; ease of access to a known document (in the case of catalogues used as a finding aid); ease of access to references on a subject; the extent to which retrieved items are relevant to the client; completeness of retrieval from the database; adequacy of content of the retrieved references; and timeliness of the service and its product.

Coverage (Completeness) of the Database

No catalogue record for material found to be in stock indicates a problem of coverage. It should be clear to potential users whether a local database covers all stock and, if not, what is excluded.[25, 80] If material is removed from stock, its record should be removed from the database or annotated as being not available locally.

In cases where relevant items known to the client are not recovered from a database during a subject search, a check search by author's name may show the reason to be poor coverage. Searchers should maintain current awareness of what subjects and types of material are covered by commercial databases in the area relevant to their clients. They should be aware of which serials are abstracted or indexed from cover to cover by a database.

Accessibility and Ease of Use

Sufficient terminals should be provided to access online databases, and space made available at the terminal for writing.[81] Access to a library catalogue from outside the library should be allowed, as should access to commercial databases from library terminals. Users should be trained and alerted to the availability of external databases. CD-ROM databases should be installed.

An explanation should be provided of how to use the system. Help screens should be written in a language a novice user can understand, and superfluous information avoided. Any error messages should tell the user what to do to recover, and be non-threatening.[82] The screen display should inform the user what he/she can do next.

Ease of Access to a Document

If items known to be in stock are requested on interlibrary loan, it may mean that clients are having difficulty in using the catalogue to locate them.

Keyword as well as name search should be made available. The system should display any variants on a name supplied by the user. An item's location in the building should be displayed, and whether or not it is on loan.

Ease of Access to References on a Subject

If users are observed to give up a search, or try an author approach for a subject search, or complain that new topics are not in the index, a failure to give due attention to ease of subject access may be responsible.

For an indexed or classified database, where the provider has control over database production, there should be consistent classification of items,[25, 73] and consistent use of indexing terms. The indexers should be trained. Indexing and classification conventions should be written down and used in the compilations of a thesaurus. An updated thesaurus should be provided with scope notes on how indexing terms have been used.[73] Specific indexing terms should be used,[25, 83] and terms should be kept up to date with changes in the subject.[17, 20, 24, 72] Updated cross-references should be provided between specific and general terms, synonyms, old and new terms, proper names, and technical names.[20, 24, 72]

When a database is not indexed with standard terms or class codes, subject access should be enhanced by providing an alphabetic list or Roget-type thesaurus of "natural language" terms from the searchable text.

Relevance of Retrieved Items

The "precision" of a search was identified as an important criterion by Bourne.[39] The "precision ratio" is the number of relevant items retrieved by the search, as a proportion of the total number retrieved. Cronin[32] suggests a target of 80 percent precision for an online search. In assessing precision, who should decide what is relevant, and on what basis has always been a problem. At one extreme, the searcher could decide, looking for items which contained the intended meaning of the search profile. At the other extreme, the client could admit items felt to be useful.

A searcher should spend enough time understanding the user's need. He/she could ask to see a relevant paper on the search topic, and use words from it in the search. If regular searches are made for a client, the client interest profile should be updated frequently. Subject knowledge in the searcher helps with precision.[84] Dolan[85] suggests testing the "cognitive style" of candidate searchers. The client could be present during a search to comment on retrieved references. Pre-search interview and search should be done by the same person.

In the search, formulation codes should be used, which limit the search to specific parts of the database—for example, class codes, or "treatment", or "operation" codes.

Selectivity[17] or specificity[86] of searches in an indexed database are improved if detailed indexing of material has been done. Schultz[87] describes skill tests for candidate indexers.

Completeness of Retrieval from Database

Kent[88] identified "recall ratio" as an important measure of the quality of reference retrieval. This is the proportion of the relevant items, held in a database which is retrieved in a search. In an experimental system, one can count the relevant items in the database. In real life, an estimate has to be made. Lancaster[1, 57] describes methods for doing this.

Consistent and exhaustive indexing is necessary to enable good recall from an indexed database. A thesaurus of indexing terms should be provided. Indexers should keep up with new ideas in the subject of the database.

A searcher with experience of the database should be used and the search made in a quiet place. The searcher should persevere with alternative search strategies. The output from a search should be examined for words which can be added to the search profile. If many terms are combined with "and" in a search, recall is reduced.

Adequacy of Retrieved References

High demand for copies of material found in commercial or local databases may indicate that the details given with references are inadequate for clients to judge the relevance of the items.

Information about each item should be added to the bibliographic record. When producing printed indexes from titles, they should be enriched with helpful terms.[73] The titles of books and reports should be supplemented with contents page information.[25, 75] In abstracts or annotations prepared for a database the scope, level and type of treatment should be indicated, as well as the main ideas from an article. An English abstract should be supplied for material in a foreign language. Abstactors should be trained to supply detailed abstracts for reports databases.[80]

Timeliness of the Service and Product

A backlog in cataloguing, abstracting or indexing for a local database would indicate problems here.

Quality Review of Current Awareness Service

Under consideration here is a current awareness service in which a scanner selects items from the primary and secondary literature with people's interests in mind, and sends them references, either as a list which everyone receives (an information bulletin), or as separate personal notifications, according to an "interest profile". The key issues for client satisfaction appear to be: adequate coverage of the area of clients' interests; selection of relevant items; timeliness of the service; adequate content of notifications; adequacy of back-up service; and ease of use.[89, 90]

Coverage of Clients' Interests

Poor coverage is indicated by a client being given consistently few or no notifications, the client finding relevant items missed by the scanners, or there being unused descriptors from the client's interest profile.

Different types of primary publication should be scanned (for example, conference proceedings and newsletters as well as journals). Abstracts or databases should be used to extend coverage.

Selection of Relevant Items

Feedback from clients that the personal notifications they receive are not relevant, and that they have found items the service has missed, can indicate poor selection by the scanners. If the client consistently receives a large number of items, or relevant items of minor importance, this can indicate poor selection.

Scanners must get to know a client's work,[31] and keep the interest profile up to date. Is there enough detail in the profile to enable the scanners to be selective? Subject knowledge helps scanners to recognize useful material. Scanners should be trained to use difficult sources and the client asked what *type* of item is needed.

Timeliness of Service

If notified items have already been seen by the client, the service may be too slow. The user should be asked *how* they were seen.

The production system should be reviewed to eliminate time wasting. Clients should be supplied with notifications or bulletins frequently enough.[39] In areas where the client needs to receive new information quickly, primary sources should be scanned.

Content of Notifications

If clients ask for copies of many of the items about which they have been notified, the notifications may not contain enough information for clients to judge the relevance of the items.[17]

Scanners should be trained in extracting information, in abstract writing, and annotation.

Adequacy of Back-up Service

A copy of the original should be available to the client soon after notification. A check should be kept on how long clients have to wait to see a notified document or receive a copy.

Items notified should be put on display. Short loans of notified material should be arranged.

Ease of Use of Service

The format of notifications should be arranged so that the titles stand out from authors, keywords, and other material. A location should be given for items, if possible, and it should be easy to order or borrow a copy. An attractive page format should be designed for bulletins, so that they stand out from other material on a client's desk. Online bulletins must not be harder to read than paper bulletins.[80] Small, frequent bulletins are less of a reading task than large ones.

Conclusion

It is so often repeated that "all libraries are different" that we tend to forget that, in one respect, they are all the same: they all give the same types of service. If we start by looking at a library as most of our clients do—as a place from where a document or copy, some information, or some references may be obtained—we may find that we already know a great deal about the appraisal of library quality. Of course, this approach to devising quality schemes for libraries does assume a willingness to make use of past findings about library services, and part and parcel of this is the willingness to accept input on service quality from our clients.

Is quality of service important enough to us to justify the expenditure of time and money on its optimization or improvement?

References

1. Lancaster, F. W., "Medlars: A Report on the Evaluation of its Operating Efficiency", *American Documentation*, Vol. 20 No. 2, 1969, pp. 119-42.

2. Orr, R. H., "Measuring the Goodness of Library Services: A General Framework for Considering Quantitative Measures", *Journal of Documentation*, Vol. 29 No. 3, 1973, pp. 315-32.

3. Rouse, W. B., "Optimal Resource Allocation in Library Systems", *Journal of the American Society for Information Science*, Vol. 26 No. 3, 1975, pp. 157-65.

4. Taylor, M. H. and Wilson, T. (Eds.), *QA: Quality Assurance in Libraries: The Health Care Sector*, Canadian Library Association, Ottawa, 1990, pp. viii-xiii.

5. *Quality Systems*, British Standards Institution, London, 1987-91, BS 5750.

6. Greenwood, J., "Setting Standards for Quality Assurance: the Canadian Experience", in Taylor, M. H. and Wilson, T. (Eds.), *QA: Quality Assurance in Libraries: The Health Care Sector*, Canadian Library Association, Ottawa, 1990, pp. 17-32.

7. Van Loo, J., "Performance Indicators in the Health Care Library: the Macro Dimension", in Taylor, M. H. and Wilson, T. (Eds.), *QA: Quality Assurance in Libraries: The Health Care Sector*, Canadian Library Association, Ottawa, 1990, pp. 65-84.

8. Gann, R., "Assuring the Quality of Consumer Health Information", in Taylor, M. H. and Wilson, T. (Eds.), *QA: Quality Assurance in Libraries: The Health Care Sector*, Canadian Library Association, Ottawa, 1990, pp. 129-46.

9. Porter, L., "Setting ILL Standards in a Nursing Library", in Taylor, M. H. and Wilson, T. (Eds.), *QA: Quality Assurance in Libraries: The Health Care Sector*, Canadian Library Association, Ottawa, 1990, pp. 113-28.

10. Schwartz, D. G. and Eakin, D., "Reference Service Standards, Performance Criteria and Evaluation", *Journal of Academic Librarianship*, Vol. 12 No. 1, 1986, pp. 4-8.

11. Rothstein, S., "The Measurement and Evaluation of Reference Service", *Library Trends*, Vol. 12 No. 3, 1964, pp. 456-72.

12. Pizer, I. H. and Cain, A.M., "Objective Tests of Library Performance", *Special Libraries*, Vol. 59 No. 9, 1968, pp. 704-11.

13. Totterdell, B. and Bird, J., *The Effective Library: Report of the Hillingdon Project on Public Library Effectiveness*, Library Association, London, 1976.

14. "Capital Planning Information", *Qualitative Assessment of Public Reference Service*, British Library Research Paper 21, British Library Research and Development Department, London, 1987.

15. Kaske, N. K., *Effectiveness of Library Operations: A Management Information Systems Approach and Application*, University of Oklahoma, Norman, Oklahoma, 1973.

16. Stradling, B., *The Quantitative Evaluation of a Public Library Service*, FLA Thesis, Library Association, London, 1966.

17. Pryor, H. E. "An Evaluation of the NASA Scientific and Technical Information Service", *Special Libraries*, Vol. 66 No. 9, 1975, pp. 515-19.

18. Whitehall, T., "Current Awareness in Education: An Evaluation of Trent Polytechnic's Education News", *Aslib Proceedings*, Vol. 37 No. 9, 1985, pp. 355-70.

19. Slater, M. *Non-use of Library/Information Resource at the Workplace*, Aslib, London, 1984.

20. Kaske, N. K. and Sanders, N. P. "Evaluating the Effectiveness of Subject Access", *Proceedings ASIS Annual Meeting*, Vol. 17, 1980, pp. 323-25.

21. Whitehall, T., "User Valuations and Resource Management for Information Services", *Aslib Proceedings*, Vol. 32 No. 2, 1980, pp. 87-101.

22. Line, M. B., "The Ability of a University Library to Provide Books Wanted by Researchers," *Journal of Librarianship*, Vol. 5 No. 1, 1973, pp. 37-51.

23. Lewis, D. E. "A Comparison between Library Holdings and Citations", *Library and Information Research News*, No. 43, 1988, pp. 18-23.

24. Quigley, H. "An Investigation of the Possible Relationships of Interbranch Loan to Cataloguing", *Library Quarterly*, Vol. 14 No. 4, 1944, pp. 333-38.

25. Lipetz, B., *User Requirements in Identifying Desired Works in a Large Library*, Yale University Library, New Haven, CT, 1970.

26. Markey, K. *The Process of Subject Searching in the Library Catalog: Final Report of the Subject Access Research Project*, Online Computer Library Center, Dublin, Ohio, 1983.

27. Van House, N. A., Lynch, M. J., McClure, C. R., Zweizig, D. L. and Roger, E. J., Output Measures for Public Libraries, American Library Association, Chicago, 1987.

28. DeProspo, E. R., Altman, E. and Beasley, K. E., Performance Measures for Public Libraries, Public Library Association, Chicago, 1973.

29. King Research, Inc., *Keys to Success: Performance Indicators for Public Libraries*, HMSO, London, 1990.

30. Moore, N., *Measuring the Performance of Public Libraries: A Draft Manual*, UNESCO, Paris, 1989.

31. Maizell, R. E., "Standards for Measuring the Effectiveness of Technical Library Performance", *Institute of Radio Engineers Transactions on Engineering Management*, EM-7, New York, 1960, pp. 69-72.

32. Cronin, M. J., *Performance Measurement for Public Services in Academic and Research Libraries*, Association of Research Libraries, Washington, DC, 1985.

33. Martin, L. A., "Commentary on Papers at a Symposium on Evaluation of Library Services", *Library Trends*, Vol. 22 No. 3, 1974, pp. 403-13.

34. Lancaster, F. W., *The Measurement and Evaluation of Library Services*, Information Resources Press, Washington, DC, 1977.

35. "Interlibrary Co-operation and Standards of Public Library Service", *Aslib Proceedings*, Vol. 15 No. 8, 1963, pp. 229-33.

36. Bunge, C.A., "Approaches to the Evaluation of Library Reference Services", in Lancaster, F. W. and Cleverdon, C. (Eds.), *Evaluation & Scientific Management of Libraries and Information Centres*, Noordhoff, Leyden, 1977, pp. 41-71.

37. Stodulski, A., "Objectives, Standards and Guidelines in the Quality Assurance Information Service", in Taylor, M. H. and Wilson, T. (Eds.), *QA: Quality Assurance in Libraries: The Health Care Sector*, Canadian Library Association, Ottawa, 1990, pp. 147-58.

38. McFarlane, L., "QA: A Personal Perspective", *Bibliotheca Medica Canadiana*, Vol. 6 No. 5, 1985, pp. 182-86.

39. Bourne, C. P. "Some User Requirements Stated Quantitatively in Terms of the 90% Library", in Kent, A. and Taulbee, O. E. (Eds.), *Electronic Information Handling*, Spartan Books, Washington, DC, 1965, pp. 93-110.

40. Duchow, S. R., "Quality Assurance for Health and Hospital Libraries: General Considerations and Background", *Bibliotheca Medica Canadiana*, Vol. 6 No. 5, 1985, pp. 177-81.

41. Potter, J., "Performance Measures: The User View", in Harris C. and Clifford, B. (Eds.), *Public Libraries: Re-appraisal and Restructuring*, Rossendale, London, 1985, pp. 111-29.

42. Griffiths, J. and King, D. W., *A Manual on the Evaluation of Information Centers and Services*, AGARD AG-310, North Atlantic Treaty Organization Advisory Group for Aerospace Research and Development, Neuilly-sur-Seine, France, 1991.

43. Institute for Operational Research, *The Scope for Operational Research in the Library and Information Field*, OSTI Report 5136, Institute for Operational Research, London, 1972.

44. Hamburg, M. "Statistical Methods for Library Management", in Chen, C.C. (Ed.), *Quantitative Measurement and Dynamic Library Service*, Oryx Press, New York, 1978, pp. 31-43.

45. Fredenburg, A.M., "Quality Assurance: Establishing a Program for Special Libraries", *Special Libraries*, Vol. 79 No. 4, 1988, pp. 277-84.

46. Eagleton, K. M., "Quality Assurance in Canadian Hospital Libraries: The Challenge of the Eighties", *Health Libraries Review*, Vol. 5 No. 3, 1988, pp. 145-59.

47. Fitzgerald, D., "Strategic Planning, the Basis for Quality Assurance", in Taylor, M. H. and Wilson, T. (Eds.), *QA: Quality Assurance in Libraries: The Health Care Sector*, Canadian Library Association, Ottawa, 1990, pp. 1-15.

48. Gillespie, S. A., "Quality Assurance Dos and Don'ts", *Bibliotheca Medica Canadiana*, Vol. 6 No. 5, 1985, pp. 187-91.

49. Whitehall, T., *Cost, Value and Effectiveness of Library & Information Service*, MPhil Thesis, Loughborough University of Technology, 1984.

50. Henderson-Stewart, D., "Performance Measurement and Review in Local Government", in Cave, M., Kogan, M., and Smith, R., *Output & Performance Measurement in Government: A State of the Art*, J. Kingsley Publishers, London, 1990, Ch. 7.

51. Weech, T. L., "Evaluation of Adult Reference Service", *Library Trends*, Vol. 22 No. 3, 1974, pp. 315-35.

52. Blick, A. R., "The Value of Measurements in Decision Making in an Information Unit", *Aslib Proceedings*, Vol. 29 No. 5, 1977, pp. 189-96.

53. Houser, L., *New Jersey Area Libraries: A Pilot Project toward the Evaluation of the Reference Collection*, New Jersey Library Association, New Brunswick, NJ, 1968.

54. Arthur, G., "Peer Coaching in a University Reference Department", *College & Research Libraries*, Vol. 51 No. 4, 1990, pp. 367-73.

55. King, G. B. and Berry, R., *Evaluation of the University of Minnesota Libraries Reference Department Telephone Information Service: Pilot Study*, University of Minnesota Library School, Minneapolis, 1973.

56. Schmidt, J., "Evaluation of Reference Service in College Libraries in New South Wales", *Library Effectiveness, A State of the Art*, Library Administration & Management Association, American Library Association, Chicago, 1980, pp. 265-94.

57. Lancaster, F. W., *If You Want to Evaluate Your Library . . .*, Library Association, London, 1938.

58. Judkins, D. Z., Hewison, N. S., Williams, S. E., Olson-Urlie, C. and Teich, C., "Standards for Reference Services in Health Science Libraries: The Reference Product", *Medical Reference Services Quarterly*, Vol. 5 No. 3, 1986, pp. 35-49.

59. Crowley, T. and Childers, T., *Information Service in Public Libraries: Two Studies*, Scarecrow Press, Methuchen, NJ, 1971.

60. Childers, T., "Managing the Quality of Reference/Information Service", *Library Quarterly*, Vol. 42 No. 2, 1972, pp. 212-17.

61. Hernon, P. and McClure, C. R., *Unobtrusive Testing and Library Reference Services*, Ablex Publishing Corporation, Norwood, NJ, 1987.

62. Shedlock, J., "Defining the Quality of Medical Reference Service", *Medical Reference Services Quarterly*, Vol. 7 No. 1, 1988, pp. 49-53.

63. Young, W. F., "Methods for Evaluating Reference Desk Performance", *RQ*, Vol. 25 No. 1, 1985, pp. 69-75.

64. Lopez, M. D. and Rubacher, R., "Interpersonal Psychology: Librarians and Patrons", *Catholic Library World*, Vol. 40 No. 8, 1969, pp. 483-87.

65. Dougherty, R. M. and Blomquist, L. L., *Improving Access to Library Resources*, Scarecrow Press, Methuchen, NJ, 1974.

66. Orr, R. H., Pings, V. M., Pizer, I. H., Olsen, E. F. and Spencer, C. P., "Development of Methodological Tools for Planning and Managing Library Services: II: Measuring a Library's Capability for Providing Documents", *Bulletin of the Medical Libraries Association*, Vol. 56 No. 3, 1968, pp. 241-67.

67. Goldhor, H., "Analysis of an Inductive Method for Evaluating the Book Collection of a Public Library", *Libri*, Vol. 23 No. 1, 1973, pp. 6-17.

68. Bonn, G. S., "Evaluation of the Collection", *Library Trends*, Vol. 22 No. 3, 1974, pp. 265-304.

69. Taylor, M. H., "Quality Assurance and Collection Evaluation", in Taylor, M. H. and Wilson, T. (Eds.), *QA: Quality Assurance in Libraries: The Health Care Sector*, Canadian Library Association, Ottawa, 1990, pp. 101-12.

70. Coale, R. P., "Evaluation of a Research Library Collection", *Library Quarterly*, Vol. 35 No. 3, 1965, pp. 173-84.

71. Swanson, D., "Requirements Study for Future Catalogs", *Library Quarterly*, Vol. 42 No. 3, 1972, pp. 302-15.

72. Jackson, S. L., *Catalog Use Study*, American Library Association, Chicago, 1958.

73. Needham, A., *User Reactions to Various Forms and Orders of Catalogue*, Bath University Library, 1974.

74. Schofield, J. L., Cooper, A. and Waters, D. H., "Evaluation of an Academic Library's Stock Effectiveness", *Journal of Librarianship*, Vol. 7 No. 3, 1975, pp. 207-27.

75. Seracevic, T., Shaw, W. M. and Kantor, P. B., "Causes and Dynamics of User Frustration in an Academic Library", *College & Research Libraries*, Vol. 38 No. 1, 1977, pp. 7-18.

76. Shaw, W. M., "Longitudinal Study of Book Availability", *Library Effectiveness: A State of the Art*, Library Administration and Management Association, Chicago, 1980, pp. 338-49.

77. Revill, D. H., "Availability as a Performance Measure for Academic Libraries", *Journal of Librarianship*, Vol. 19 No. 1, 1987, pp. 14-30.

78. Buckland, M., *Book Availability and the Library User*, Pergamon Press, Oxford, 1975.

79. Hoffman, A. C., "Monograph Duplication in the Kresge Center for Teaching Resources at Lesley College", in Chen, C.C. (Ed.), *Quantitative Measurement and Dynamic Library Service*, Oryx Press, New York, 1978, pp. 225-44.

80. Archibald, G., Dissertation for Diploma in Professional Studies, Loughborough University of Technology, 1988, pp. 15-42.

81. Markey, K., *Subject Searching in Library Catalogs—Before and After the Introduction of Online Catalogs*, OCLC Online Computer Library Center Inc., Dublin, Ohio, 1984.

82. Coats, R. B. and Vlaeminke, I., *Man-Computer Interfaces: An Introduction to Software Design and Implementation*, Blackwell, Oxford, 1987.

83. Perrine, R. H., "Catalog Use Difficulties", *RQ*, Vol. 7 No. 4, 1968, pp. 169-74.

84. Van Camp, A., "Effective Search Analysts", *Online*, Vol. 3 No. 2, 1979, pp. 18-20.

85. Dolan, D. R. and Kremin, M. C., "The Quality Control of Search Analysts", *Online*, Vol. 3 No. 2, 1979, pp. 8-16.

86. Kiewitt, E. L., *Evaluating Information Retrieval Systems: The PROBE Program*, Greenwood Press, Westport, CT, 1979.

87. Schultz, C. K., "Performance Measures for Libraries and Information Centers", in Slater, F. (Ed.), *Cost Reduction for Special Libraries and Information Centers*, American Society for Information Science, Washington, DC, 1973, pp. 139-51.

88. Kent, A., "Machine Literature Searching: VIII: Operational Criteria for Designing IR Systems", *American Documentation*, Vol. 6 No. 2, 1955, pp. 93-101.

89. Whitehall, T., *Personal Current Awareness Service: A Handbook of Techniques for Manual SDI*, British Library R&D Report 5502, British Library Research and Development Department, London, 1979.

90. Whitehall, T., *Practical Current Awareness Service from Libraries*, Gower, Aldershot, 1986, Ch. 7.

PART II
Quality Management in Libraries: A Select Bibliography

Select Bibliography

(The articles reprinted in this sourcebook are noted with an *.)

The literature in the area of TQM and quality assurance, control, management, services, and so on, is exploding before our eyes. This select bibliography reflects searches in *Library & Information Science Abstracts (LISA)*, *Library Literature*, and CARL's UnCover databases through December 21, 1993. I also followed through on many of the references cited in these articles and scanned TQM-rich library journals, adding some recently published (but as of this writing unindexed) titles.

Also included are unannotated citations found in the bibliographies of other works. (They appear unannotated here due to the lateness of my discovering them.)

Much literature can be found on quality assurance, control, management, and so on, from the United Kingdom. I attained as much as I could without going to England myself to get them (or totally alienating my Interlibrary Loan Department). I have also noted in the annotations the bibliographies and references that are particularly rich in additional resources.

Albritton, Rosie L., and Thomas W. Shaughnessy. *Developing Leadership Skills: A Source Book for Librarians.* Englewood, Colo.: Libraries Unlimited, 1990.

While this book does not address TQM or continuous quality improvement specifically, it does address one of the qualities required in a good total quality manager: good leadership skills. Composed of articles by some of the top administrators in our profession, it covers the gamut of personal development, such as communication skills, managing conflict, the differences between manager and leader, time management, and women as leaders. It also provides exercises and inventories to assist leaders in judging their potential as leaders, their assertiveness quotient, and attitude toward conflict, to name a few.

Allan, Ferne C. "Benchmarking: Practical Aspects for Information Professionals." *Special Libraries* 84, no. 3 (Summer 1993):123-130.

Provides an overview of the benchmarking process in light of the Malcolm Baldrige National Quality Award, industry practices, and benchmarking application (a 12-step process) at Sandia Laboratories that includes a benchmarking department. Offers advice on the role of the information professional in this process and basic guidelines for involvement.

125

Annichiarico, Mark. "Baker & Taylor's Coup de Grace." *Library Journal* 118, no. 11 (September 15, 1993):44-46.

Describes some of the benefits, both financial and in efficiencies that B&T has experienced by adopting TQM principles. One change is to now describe itself "as a provider of information and entertainment services rather than simply a distributor" (p.44).

*Armstrong, Barbara. "Libraries Around Australia: Introducing Total Quality Management to Telecom's National Resource Centre." *Australian Library Journal* 40, no. 4 (November 1991):349-354.

This is one of the earliest thorough articles in library literature that addresses the implementation of TQM in a library system. The author considers initial confusion regarding this new practice understandable and stresses the importance of bringing those involved up to speed. The article is very useful in providing guidance on setting the stage for TQM before actual implementation. For example, Telecom hired a TQM coordinator (Armstrong) and circulated a paper to all staff that explained the concepts and approaches of this program. Areas studied included inputting of records into the local catalog, and interlibrary loans.

Avery, Christine, and Diane Zabel. "TQM: A Primer." *RQ* 32, no. 2 (Winter 1993):206-216.

This "primer" is aimed at orienting the profession to primary materials on total quality management, concentrating on public sector institutions rather than the manufacturing world where TQM originated. It addresses six basic philosophies of TQM such as zeroing in on the process, not the people, as the culprits of quality deficiencies; empowering employees; and the customer as focus. The article includes 24 general resources, 22 on specific aspects of TQM, and 6 others specifically from the service industry. Also shares a list of subject headings and quality-rich databases to use for further research, as well as the names and addresses of specific organizations.

Baker, Sharon L., and F. Wilfrid Lancaster. *The Measurement and Evaluation of Library Services*. 2d ed. Arlington, Va.: Information Resources Press, 1991.

A departure from the first edition (Lancaster, 1977), this textbook covers the evaluations of public services only. From page xvi of the preface: "...concentrates on the evaluation of collections and materials availability, certain types of reference services (including database searching), and catalog use, as well as the effects of accessibility and ease of use on public services, the range and scope of library services, the relevance of standards to evaluation activities, and evaluation by means of user studies." Extensive bibliographies follow each chapter and it is generously illustrated. While, according to the index, this monograph does not mention TQM, it is intended to assist libraries in the evaluation of the effectiveness and efficiency of their public (i.e., customer) service, and therefore may prove useful for data collection.

Barnard, Susan B. "Implementing Total Quality Management: A Model for Research Libraries." *Journal of Library Administration* 18, no. 1/2 (1993):57-70.

Presents a model for implementing TQM in a research library based on her work with the Association of Research Libraries' Office of Management Services on bringing these concepts and training opportunities to research libraries. Includes a 10-step process (in four phases); good references.

*———. "Total Quality Management: Customer-Centered Models for Libraries." *ARL* no. 158 (September 25, 1991):4-6.

This brief look at TQM provides a theoretical description of what TQM can bring to an institution, and in particular addresses its potential for research libraries. It notes the importance of empowerment and how its effectiveness is contingent on a cultural transformation. It's a good, quick overview for those who are unfamiliar with the processes and philosophies of total quality management.

Benchmarking, Total Quality Management, and the Learning Organization. Special Libraries 84, no. 3 (Summer 1993):120-157.

Guy St. Clair, editor of this special issue, briefly introduces the distinguished group of writers (p.120-122) and also closes the package off with an extensive bibliography (p.155-157). The issue covers areas such as benchmarking, quality assurance, measurements of quality, and a case study. Each article is also reviewed separately. This title represents a portion of the Summer, 1993 issue of *Special Libraries* which was dedicated to these topics.

Berner, Andrew. "Thinking About ... Quality." *The One-Person Library* 6, no. 8 (December 1989):6-7.

A thought piece on the pursuit of excellence. Not worth the interlibrary loan charges if you don't subscribe.

Bial, Raymond. "Quality Circles in a Community College LRC." *Community and Junior College Libraries* 3, no. 2 (Winter 1984):27-31.

The application of quality circles took place at Parkland College in Champaign, Illinois, in the early 1980s and is an example of the success of the quality tools and quality circles in a smaller library setting. These circles had three objectives: 1) brainstorm ideas for problems to be solved and select one by consensus to solve; 2) identify the most effective solution to the problem; and 3) implement the solution. The teams' effectiveness in communication and creativity was important and they followed the DOVE guide for brainstorming: Do not judge ideas; One person in turn; Variety in thinking is important; Energize the group with creative thoughts. Author also recommends a discussion of up front communication, both internal and external, for good communication is essential to the success of these circles. Includes the survey used.

Blagden, John, and John Harrington. *How Good Is Your Library? A Review of Approaches to the Evaluation of Library and Information Services*. London: Aslib, 1990.

Offers a literary overview (from 1982 to present) of the many approaches to the evaluation of library and information services. Includes
an extensive bibliography. They cover, for example, cost benefit analysis,
peer review, unobtrusive testing, and case histories.

Brockman, John R. "Information Management and Corporate Total Quality."
Journal of Information Science 19, no. 4 (1992):259-266.
Examines the relationships between information management (IM)
and total quality (TQ) and how they have evolved from the productivity-
oriented management philosophy of the past to the present customer-
driven philosophy. The various quality awards worldwide are noted with
special focus on the criteria of the Malcolm Baldrige National Quality
Award through which he examines the role of information management
in the total quality organization. (*Cf.* Galvin's "Quality: The New Imperative" and Ojala's "Quality Online and Online Quality.")

*———. "Just Another Management Fad? The Implications of TQM for
Libraries and Information Services." *Aslib Proceedings* 78, no. 7/8
(July/August 1992):283-288.
Presents an overview of the library and information services and its
move from quality control, through the uses of quality assurance, to
today's applications of quality management. While it leans more heavily
in the direction of British libraries and British Standards certification, it
has considerable practical information to share, including a graphical
study of library literature. It notes several success stories and heralds the
Canadian medical libraries as "QA pioneers."

———. "Quality Assurance (QA) and the Management of Information Services."
Journal of Information Science 17, no. 2 (June 1991):127-135.
Reports from a one-day seminar in England covering "the history of
QA, reasons for its adoption, steps for implementation, the importance of
standards, contractual aspects, training needs, the identification of user
needs and user feedback, and the implications arising from the introduction of a QA programme." While the day-long program was probably more
fulfilling, this account is quite detailed and worth reading.

———. "Quality Management in Library and Information Services in the
Washington Area." *Library and Information Research News* 14, no. 52
(Winter 1991):6-11.
Reflects the interim findings of an investigation of the feasibility of TQM
applications in library and information services in the United States and the
United Kingdom. Focuses on experiences of TQM application in the U.S.
federal government libraries with mention of academics and one public.

Brophy, Peter, Kate Coulling, and Maxine Melling. "Quality Management: A University Approach." *Aslib Information* 21, no. 6 (June
1993):246-248.
The official British Standard defines quality as "the totality of features
and characteristics of a product or service that bear on its ability to satisfy
stated or implied needs" (p. 246). However, the approach taken by this

university was based on what they considered a more reasonable approach: "The closest fit to users' needs that resources permit" (p.246). Based on this premise, the authors offer their prescription for quality management based on a combination of quality management systems, including BS 5750.

Butcher, Karyle. "Total Quality Management: The Oregon State University Library's Experience." *Journal of Library Administration* 18, no. 1/2 (1993):45-56.
Oregon State University was one of the first higher education institutions to implement TQM institution wide. This article documents the experiences of the university libraries.

Byrne, David. "Delivering Quality Services Through Technology: Contributions from the Legal Information Professional." *The Law Librarian* 24, no. 1 (March 1993):26-29.
Research based on the results of a questionnaire querying information professionals, Byrne seeks to draw conclusions on how and why technology can make significant, value-added differences in service quality. The author also briefly addresses the state of the art of telecommunications and concludes that technology must result from dialogue between user and supplier and be customer-driven rather than technology led.

——. "Quality Management in Library and Information Services." *The Law Librarian* 24, no. 2 (June 1993):69-74.
Brief overview of TQM including a comparison with BS 5750. Applies, albeit briefly, the elements of the Malcolm Baldrige National Quality Award to the library setting. Updates overall status of TQM in the United Kingdom, and supplies an extensive bibliography, of which a large percentage are U.K. imprints.

Campbell, Corinne A. "Information Services at Boeing: Adding Values by Measuring and Improving Quality." In *Online / CDROM '92 Conference Proceedings, Washington, D.C., October 26-28, 1992.* Wilton, Conn.: Eight Bit Books, 1992.
Documents the implementation of CQI (continuous quality improvement) at Boeing Technical Libraries. Based on the results of a detailed task analysis, verification of customer requirements, and prioritization of the issues raised, the staff focuses on four key areas for improvement: reducing flow time, offering alternatives to microfiche and other microfilm products, improving information access, and increasing efforts to filter and focus information to meet each customer's specific needs. Describes how each was approached and shares ideas for future directions.

Carr, Stephen J. "Strategic Planning in Libraries." *Library Management* 13, no. 5 (1992):4-17.
An excellent step-by-step description and guide to strategic planning in libraries. Includes assistance in the mission and goals and objectives aspect, but is not as strong in the area of "vision." Coupled with Riggs' chapter reprinted here from *Advances in Librarianship*, library managers are well-prepared for crafting their own strategic plans after reading this

article. It includes a fine bibliography for additional library management research.

Clack, Mary Elizabeth. "Organizational Development and TQM: The Harvard College Library's Experience." *Journal of Library Administration* 18, no. 1/2 (1993):29-43.
Describes the process whereby Harvard University Libraries has begun to pilot a TQM program and provide library-wide training.

Clayton, Carl. "Quality and the Public Services." *Public Library Journal* 8, no. 1 (January/February 1993):11-12.
An editorial directed as a response to a 1992 Bob Usherwood article on public library services (see Usherwood's "Managing Public Libraries as a Public Service"). Doesn't add much to the library literature except that for libraries who have easy access to some of the titles in the references provided, this piece could be quite useful. Includes response from Usherwood.

Clayton, Peter. "Japanese Management Theory and Library Administration." *Journal of Academic Librarianship* 18, no. 5 (November 1992):298-301.
While TQM plays only a brief role in this particular article, the Japanese style of management is one of the reasons TQM has been successful in Japan, making this style important to understand as we implement TQM in American libraries. The author notes the three pillars of this management approach: 1) lifetime employment; 2) seniority plus merit pay; and 3) enterprise unions (not skill-oriented, but rather, linked to the organization). Because libraries tend to be short-term and reactive in their decision making, consensual decision making needs to become more prevalent. We also need to listen more intently to the "stakeholders" of our libraries: the patrons. The author also addresses the differences between quality control and quality assurance.

Comola, Jackie. "The Human Side of Management." *Executive Housekeeping Today* 12, no. 10: (October 1, 1991):7.
While this article doesn't come from the library literature, it offers a very useful list of 23 questions (taken from the Human Resources Utilization section of the Malcolm Baldrige National Quality Award criteria) that can be used to assess how well an organization is addressing the human side of quality.

Curtis, Michael, Sue Wheeler, Linna White, and Barbara Jennings. "Quality Assurance in Kent." *Public Library Journal* 8, no. 1 (January/February 1993):1-4.
Describes the quality assurance program at the Kent Arts and Libraries Department in Kent, England, a county-wide service effort. Outlines the process for standards creation, monitoring, support for their efforts, and the outline for quality awareness training. Good example for a multi-branch library setting.

Dawes, Susan. "A Service of Quality." *Aslib Information* 20, no. 6 (June 1992):250-251.
Presents both the pluses and the minuses of BS 5750 accreditation and record keeping.

Dawson, Andy. "Quality First! The Taywood Information Centre and BS 5750." *Aslib Information* 20, no. 1 (March 1992):112-113.
A BS 5750 accreditation success story.

Dee, Bernard E. *Total Quality Management: Performance Standards for Today's Information Managers*. Alabama: Maxwell Air Force Base, 1990.
Not library-related, but interesting from an information-flow vantage point.

DeSirey, Janice, et al. "The Quality Circle: Catalyst for Library Change." *Library Journal* 113, no. 7 (April 15, 1988):52-53.
These authors document the mid-1980s application of quality circles at the Hennepin County Library. They established two circles, one with cataloging staff, the other with processing staff. The cataloging QC addressed the cataloging backlog, experienced great success, and later took on other tasks to study. Within its first year, however, the processing QC disbanded due to personality difficulties.

Diggins, Nyree. "Total Quality Management and the Special Librarian." *Achieving Excellence: Proceedings of the 4th Asian Pacific Special and Law Librarians Conferences....* Canberra, Australia: Special Libraries and Health Libraries Sections, ALIA, and Australian Law Librarians Group, 1991.
This paper focuses on the special librarian as implementer and partner in the TQM program of his or her organization. Diggins offers assistance to the special librarian on understanding how TQM should be understood and applied, especially if being adopted by the parent organization. Diggins sees TQM as the vehicle for librarians to "increase their perceived significance to the business as not only an information specialist but also a customer analysis specialist." These intangibles include "improved decision making, competitive advantage and infrastructure support."

DiMattia, Ernest A. "Total Quality Management and Servicing Users Through Remote Access Technology." *The Electronic Library* 11, no. 3 (June 1993):187-192.
After a brief overview of prescriptions of the quality gurus Deming and Juran, this article seeks to assist libraries in maintaining that competitive edge in information provision. The author believes that if we don't provide quality service, others will enter our market and provide the service our customers seek. He considers personnel, user communication, equipment support, and providing the product mix the customer seeks as the keys to success. Other factors are also noted and discussed. An excellent practical piece on services to remote users.

Dougherty, Richard M. "TQM: Is It the Real Thing?" (editorial). *Journal of Academic Librarianship* 18, no. 3 (March 1992):3.

This editorial is a good food for thought contribution to the literature. Dougherty highlights aspects of the TQM philosophy that can so obviously apply to libraries and makes several good points in that regard. For example, "our products (i.e., our nonhuman resources) and our services (e.g., ILL, reference, circulation) are often sources of patron dissatisfaction and complaint. And, if we expand our view to consider how well we satisfy those other 'customers'—the academic administrators who allocate library funds—it should also be clear that there is room for improvement." Dougherty believes it could just be a fad, or it could be just what the library profession needs to do the introspection necessary to succeed in understanding what our customers truly need and then meeting (and surpassing) that need.

Duffeck, Elizabeth, and Warren Harding. "Quality Management in the Military: An Overview and a Case Study." *Special Libraries* 84, no. 3 (Summer 1993):137-141.

Offers a case study of quality improvement initiatives at the United States Department of Defense. Shares the multi-linked teams' TQM organizational structure at the Naval Air Systems Command, how this structure served as a catalyst for change at the Research Library, and the effect on the Library's budget and funding.

Eagleton, Kathleen M. "Quality Assurance in Canadian Hospitals—The Challenge of the Eighties." *Health Libraries Review* 5 (1988):145-159.

Documents the history of Canadian and American hospital accreditation and includes as an appendix the accreditation guidelines for Canadian hospital libraries as of 1986. Eagleton discusses the quality assurance programs that evolved in response to the evolving standards in accreditation of Canadian health care facilities, and offers a good, selected bibliography on quality assurance programs in Canadian and American special libraries.

Emolo, Lauren M. "Assessing Upper Management." *SpeciaList* 15, no. 2 (December 1992):1-2.

Reflects an interview with Dr. Christine Pearson in anticipation of her presentation at the 1993 Winter Education Conference. Very brief. Better time is spent reading Pearson's article ("Aligning TQM and Organizational Learning") based on that presentation in the Summer 1993 issue of *Special Libraries*.

Euster, Joanne R., et al. "Quality Circles: New Approaches to an Old Game." (Program Panel presented by the Association of College and Research Libraries, Community and Junior College Library Section of the American Library Association. 1984 ALA Annual Conference, June 23-27, Dallas, Texas.) (Two sound cassettes.)

This program, lasting approximately three hours, consists of five excellent speakers: Euster, Sell and Mortola (see their article which is based on their presentation on p. 34), Crocker, and Sannwald. Euster covers organizational dynamics in her opening remarks. Sell and Mortola provide an extensive program on quality circles, their definition, implementation, quality circle tools, and pluses and minuses. Crocker provides a two-phased reaction to Sell and Mortola that includes 10 reasons why quality circles fail and an excellent look at the Japanese work ethic (how it differs from the American work ethic), and why quality circles have worked in Japan because of that ethic. At the San Diego Public Library, Sannwald implemented an "organizational effectiveness program" that included savings of over $200,000 and the first time in SDPL history that the entire cataloging backlog was eliminated, and this due to the cooperative efforts of the staff in affecting productivity changes. That year, Sannwald's library was also getting 20 new positions that he believes was a direct result of the program.

Ferguson, Jeffrey M., and Robert A. Zawachi. "Service Quality: A Critical Success Factor for IS Organizations." *Information Strategy* 9, no. 2 (Winter 1993).
This article has been included for several reasons. First, it can be of use to those who have dual library and information services (IS) responsibilities. It can also serve graduate students getting a degree or minor in IS. As well, those who would like to assist their IS departments in improving their service quality might consider sharing this article with them, especially if you as a customer wish they would shift from technical orientation to customer orientation. Defines technical versus functional quality. Provides guidelines and a checklist to assist IS directors in moving to a successful service strategy.

*Fischer, Wenda Webster, and Linda B. Reel. "Total Quality Management (TQM) in a Hospital Library: Identifying Service Benchmarks." *Bulletin of the Medical Library Association* 80, no. 4 (October 1992):347-352.
Results of a survey conducted by the authors from which they established TQM benchmarks for service. (The survey itself is not included, but there is an address provided for requesting a copy.) Details are given of the methodology and results of the study. As in all TQM environments, the authors note that successful improvement of services will depend upon the institution's commitment to the process and willingness to change. Survey not included, but can be requested.

Fitch, Donna K., Jean Thomason, and Elizabeth Crabtree Wells. "Turning the Library Upside Down: Reorganization Using Total Quality Management Principles." *Journal of Academic Librarianship* 19, no. 5 (November 1993):294-299.
Documents Samford University's library-wide reorganization with TQM at the heart. Following the four basic principles of backing up everything with facts, avoiding feelings and emotional reasons, striving to reach a consensus, and allowing the dean to make the decision if consensus couldn't be reached, the library went from a traditional organizational structure to a circular one, unwittingly à la Peter Drucker's "information-based organization." Interesting approach to resource management and hiring.

Foreman, Lewis, ed. *Developing Quality in Libraries: Culture and Measurement for Information Services.* London: HMSO, 1992. [Based on a book review by David Byrne in *The Law Librarian* 24, no. 1 (March 1993):48-49.]
This booklet represents the proceedings from the annual conference of Government Librarians, with additional offerings from Brockman and Schoolbred. References are considered good for further reading. While the reviewer considers this a "concise, low-cost introduction to the concepts and current trends in quality issues," and recommends it as a "useful introduction," he disagrees with their definitions of quality.

Frank, Robyn C. "Total Quality Management: The Federal Government Experience." *Journal of Library Administration* 18, no. 1/2 (1993):171-182.
Describes the positive changes that have occurred with the impetus of TQM initiatives.

Fredenburg, Anne M. "Quality Assurance: Establishing a Program for Special Libraries." *Special Libraries* 79, no. 4 (Fall 1988):277-284.
Details the Sheppard-Pratt Hospital Library's implementation of a quality assurance program, including their problem-solving model. It provides 10 suggestions for establishing a QA program in a special library setting.

Galvin, Carol. "Quality: The New Imperative." *Marketing Library Services: MLS* 5, no. 1 (1991):4-6.
Illustrates how libraries can use the Malcolm Baldrige National Quality Award as a guide for defining quality in their libraries and to establish a quality management strategy. When combined with the Brockman (1993) and Ojala (1993) articles, provides a good, overall picture of the award and its usefulness in quality programs.

Gapen, D. Kaye, Queen Hampton, and Sharon Schmitt. "TQM: The Director's Perspective." *Journal of Library Administration* 18, no. 1/2 (1993):15-28.
Argues for TQM in research libraries and illustrates how Case Western Reserve University in Cleveland, Ohio, implemented it. Notes provide additional background reading.

Gottesman, Zmira. "Total Quality Management and Its Application in a Corporate One-Man Library." *ISLIC Bulletin* 18, no. 2: (April 1992):11-14. (In Hebrew.) [Based on a *LISA* abstract (August 1992):15]
This information specialist applies TQM in an environment where, it appears, he is the only librarian. He empowers his staff to do their best, take risks, and provide optimal customer service. He also suggests specific solutions to user needs within the library setting.

Green, Andrew. "What Do We Mean By User Needs?" *British Journal of Academic Librarianship* 5, no. 2 (1990):65-78.
The essential characteristics of "need" are detailed as well as distinguished from "wants" or "demands." Addresses the question: Who should define user needs? The professional librarian or the library user? Argues against leaving it solely in the hands of the so-called experts. Walks

through a hypothetical needs assessment based on a particular "needology." Of note, Green believes "being aware of the distinction between expressed demand and unexpressed need can save the library from more serious errors. A situation in which well-organised and articulate faculty members ventilate their own demands at frequent intervals, while the less confident voices of scattered undergraduates are heard only rarely, is all too likely to lead to attention and resources being devoted to the former at the expense of the latter" (p.66). Considers a user needs assessment a critical tool when establishing academic library policies.

*Hanks, Nancy, and Stan Wade. "Quality Circles: Realistic Alternatives for Libraries." *Show-Me Libraries* 36 (June 1985):6-11.
One of the earlier articles on the application of this quality tool, the authors provide seven detailed steps for establishing and utilizing quality circles. Emphasizes the importance of making clear the function of the circles up front and of providing all participants with proper training. Notes the need for a clear problem statement and how to reach it (though not in great detail), and gives examples of a study using some of the standard quality tools such as the fishbone diagram and force-field analysis. Good, practical article for the basics of establishing teams and making them work.

Hansel, Patsy J. "Quantity Is Not Necessarily Quality: A Challenge to Librarians to Develop Meaningful Standards of Performance for Library Reference Services." *North Carolina Libraries* 48 (Fall 1990):184-187.
Hansel believes that "as a profession we should no longer be content to assume that our libraries are giving good service" (p. 187). She discusses the value of the unobtrusive study approach and provides proof of its success in this area using two different approaches: the Wisconsin-Ohio Reference Evaluation Project, and the work of Ralph Gers and Lillie Seward at the Maryland State Library. She believes that "many reference administrators continue to object to the use of unobtrusive testing on ethical grounds. What I personally find unethical is advertising a service that is often of questionable quality" (p.185).

Hawkins, Katherine W. "Implementing Team Management in the Modern Library." *Library Administration & Management* 4, no. 1 (Winter 1990):11-15.
This article describes two kinds of management styles: mechanistic (hierarchical structure of control, authority, and communication), and organic (a network structure of control, authority, and communication). Hawkins suggests that the organic organizational structure, given the current flux in the economic environment in most libraries, is the most effective form. Also addressed is the Weberian management theory. The latter theory, which espouses the mechanistic style, is contrasted with team management theory. Hawkins discusses in detail the following communications skills she considers necessary for team management to succeed: effective delegation, balancing demands for task and social maintenance, encouraging participation and creativity, effective feedback, and sustaining behavioral change.

Henry, Barbara J. "Continuous Quality Improvement in the Hospital Library." *Bulletin of the Medical Library Association* 81, no. 4 (October 1993):437-439.

Using a survey instrument adapted from several surveys in an MLA publication, this article documents the results of a survey on their customers that had a surprising 65.3 percent response rate, the highest rate of return they had ever received on any survey. This was after quality assurance practices had been in place.

Hicks, John. "Customer Care in Berkshire." *Aslib Information* 20, no. 6 (June 1992):242-243.

Based on the premise that the library customer now has a choice of other methods of recreation and information, the Berkshire County Library System in England established a "customer care campaign" through which expectations are documented and then followed through on based on clear objectives in their annual business plan. The process of "care" is bottom-up. There is a "users charter" and a "complaints procedure." The former is supplemented by a "service promise" delineating guaranteed services, all of which are published widely. Worth reading for further ideas they've used in their campaign.

Howell, Pamela B., and Christiane J. Jones. "A Focus on Quality—The Library's Role in Occurrence Screening." *Medical Library Services Quarterly* 12, no. 2 (Summer 1993):83-89.

Specifically geared to hospital libraries and occurrence screening (defined on p. 85 of the article as "a quality assurance technique in which 'all patient care is reviewed ... against a set of general outcome screening criteria. Adverse patient occurrences are identified, confirmed by peers, trended and appropriately followed up' "). A good response to forging new roles for the medical librarians in a QA environment. A few additional articles are noted for further reading on occurrence screening.

Humphries, Anne Wood, and Gretchen V. Naisawald. "Developing a Quality Assurance Program for Online Services." *Bulletin of the Medical Library Association* 79, no. 3 (July 1991):263-270.

Provides a detailed account of how the Claude Moore Health Science Library at the University of Virginia developed a QA program centered around five determinants of customer services quality: reliability, responsiveness, assurance, empathy, and tangibles. Although these determinants come from surveys conducted in the banking, credit card, and machine repair businesses, they easily created a cadre for a QA program for the online services provided by this library. The authors believe that the quality assurance model can be useful in the evaluation of library services and that QA can be applied in specific library service areas to improve performance and experience high quality results.

Irving, Ann. "Quality in Academic Libraries: How Shall We Know It?" *Aslib Information* 20, no. 6 (June 1992):244-246.

A small study was conducted at Loughborough University to analyze the true, root cause of user problems in finding the information they seek and the effectiveness of using the services of the library. The approach was triangular in nature: tracing the problem from the student to the lecturer to the librarian. For example, a user cannot find author entries in the catalog. The student's role: recalling instructions. The catalog's role: better guiding mechanisms. Organization and management's role: better author control structure. Academic (lecturer) role: providing citations that match the entries of the OPAC. The librarian's role: being more accessible and approachable. Other examples given as well. Great approach to problem resolution.

Johannsen, C. G. "Danish Experiences of TQM in the Library World." *New Library World* 93, no. 1104:4-9 (1992).

This is one of the better articles from the international front. It deals with the progress toward TQM (i.e., from inspection-based systems, to quality control, to quality assurance, and then the pinnacle, TQM). While it folds in the EN 29000 (ISO 9000) European quality legislations, the study of the awareness of TQM principles within the library and information services arena in Denmark can easily be applied to any nation. The results of the survey used in this article is being folded into a three-country study that will be an EC project titled, "Quality Management in the Information and Library Field." One of the interesting driving forces behind quality management is the liability of libraries in our litigious society.

——. "The Use of Quality Control Principles and Methods in Library and Information Science Theory and Practice." *Libri* 42, no. 4 (October/December 1992):283-295.

Addresses the problems involved in the application of quality control and TQM principles and systems in the library and information services arena. A very thorough article with definitions and practical applications and useful references.

Johnson, Peggy. "Automation, Adaptability, and Empowerment in Technical Services." *Technicalities* 11, no. 6 (June 1991):6-9.

According to Johnson, "to be successful, contemporary organizations must be able to adjust and adapt as technologies, budgets, and client expectations change" (p.6). To achieve this end, libraries must move away from the bureaucratic structures that stifle the ability to adapt quickly. She believes automation is a driving force for organizational change in libraries because it results in empowerment, a direct result of the decentralization of decision-making inherent in automation. Staff members, in an automated environment, will be expected to exercise more responsibility and must therefore be empowered to act.

*Jurow, Susan."TQM: The Customer Focus." *ARL Current Issues* no. 158 (September 25, 1991):12.
Discusses the differences between being client-centered (getting information about what the client wants and fulfilling those expectations) and service-oriented (meeting what the librarian perceives as the patrons' needs). Jurow considers total quality management a useful tool in assessing what the patron truly needs and for improvement in the quality of library services.

Jurow, Susan, and Susan B. Barnard, guest eds. "Integrating Total Quality Management in a Library Setting." *Journal of Library Administration* 18, no. 1/2 (1993).
This was the first full monograph to appear in the library literature addressing TQM applications in libraries. Fourteen chapters in all, 11 are specifically geared toward the theoretical and practical in the library arena. Preceded by a brief TQM overview, it provides the experiences and ideas for implementing as well as supporting TQM initiatives. It is divided into the following categories: "Library Approaches to [TQM]"; "Implementing a [TQM] Program"; "Supporting [TQM] Efforts, and Learning from the Experiences of Others." Contains particularly good chapters on TQM training (pp. 85-95), and on problem-solving methods (pp. 97-112). If you're involved in TQM, your library should own this.

———. "Introduction: TQM Fundamentals and Overview of Contents." *Journal of Library Administration* 18, no. 1/2 (1993):1-13.
Introduces the above volume, including a brief overview of TQM.

———. "Tools for Measuring and Improving Performance." *Journal of Library Administration* 18, no. 1/2 (1993):113-126.
Provides examples (and illustrations) of the various tools used in the review of processes from a systems approach, including the Shewhart Cycle, flowcharts, Cause and Effect Diagram ("Fishbone"), Pareto Chart, statistical process control chart, and benchmarking.

Keiser, Barbie E. "Evaluation: An Ongoing Process." *National Online Meeting 1991, Proceedings of the 12th National Online Meeting, New York, 7-9 May, 1991.* Edited by Martha E. Williams, 179-182. Medford, N.J.: Learned Information, 1991.
Espouses the importance of product evaluation and customer feedback for continuous improvement. Gives basic overview of evaluation process and procuring feedback.

———. "Quality Assurance: A Management Challenge for the 1990s." *National Online Meeting 1990, Proceedings of the 11th National Online Meeting, New York, 1-3 May 1990.* Edited by Martha E. Williams, 193-199. Medford, N.J.: Learned Information, 1990.
A prolific author on this topic, Keiser sees the changes in economics, management techniques, and technology as having a drastic effect on the library setting, regardless of type. As these change so does the responsibility of the information gatherer to be as efficient and as accurate as

possible. Keiser states the keys to full customer service are librarians understanding what is needed and why it's needed. She suggests partnering with our vendors to provide high-quality databases, and an outreach program that might encompass workshops, newsletters, or memos.

———. "Quality Management for Libraries: A North American Perspective." *Aslib Information* 21, no. 6 (June 1993):252-255.
    Based on a presentation at an international conference on documentation, this author recommends applying the Malcolm Baldrige Award's Core Values and Concepts to the library environment. Focuses on customer-driven quality and suggests that a library must redesign its operations based on an external rather than an internal customer focus. Keiser provides valuable guidance on getting to the root of true customer needs, dealing with library competitors, and increasing the library's market share. How a library deals with complaints (opportunity versus inconvenience) indicates whether or not it is customer driven. "When customers are complaining, they are letting you know that you still have a chance to keep their business" (p.254). A must read.

Keys to Success: Performance Indicators for Public Libraries: A Manual of Performance Measures and Indicators. Developed by King Research. London: HMSO, 1990. (Library Information Series).

Koulopoulos, Thomas M. "The Document Factory." Parts 1 and 2. *Inform* 7, nos. 6 and 7 (June and July 1993):42-46, 44-47.
    This entry may come as a surprise because at first glance it doesn't seem to fit, but with the TQM process so focused on workflow analysis, this article is worth reading. It focuses on workflow, TQM, and re-engineering in the handling of information.

Lawes, Ann. "The Benefits of Quality Management to the Library and Information Services Profession." *Special Libraries* 84, no. 3 (Summer 1993):142-146.
    Addresses the importance of quality assurance in library services and how its application benefits all sectors of the information chain, including the relationship between the library and the parent organization. Concludes by saying that "in the past, there was a clear assumption that the way to improve quality [in libraries] was to consume more resources, to buy more books, recruit more staff and finally, to move to larger premises." She considers this approach no longer valid due to changes in economic and political climates. Believes that we must now become proactive rather than reactive to administrative mandate. That it, we must now initiate the mandate through quality assurance initiatives.

Lee, Hye Kyung, and Mary T. Kim. "The Relationship Between Quality of Goal Setting and Job Satisfaction in a Public Library Setting." *Public Library Quarterly* 13, no. 2 (April 1993):41-57.
    A survey of public library job satisfaction performed on 12 of 21 branch libraries in a larger metropolitan public library. Results indicate correlation

between satisfaction and goal setting. This article is included because of the goal setting aspect of TQM. Extensive bibliography.

Lewis, David W. "Eight Truths for Middle Managers in Lean Times." *Library Journal* 116, no. 14 (September 1, 1991):157-158.
Although this article never once mentions TQM (it does mention quality, though), the "eight truths" it offers easily fold into what a quality manager must face. Many skeptics of TQM use the "bottom line" of the corporate world to excuse them from TQM initiatives, but as Lewis notes as truth #2, "it is a zero sum game" and making the best use of resources is every manager's responsibility, as is being willing to change. A good read.

Liu, Xuefeng. "The Application of the Cause Effect Diagram with Addition of Cards to Library Management." *Chung-kuo tu shu kuan hsueh pao* (*Bulletin of the Chinese Libraries*) 19, no. 1 (1993):85- [Original text in Chinese.]
Describes use of CEDAC (Cause and Effect Diagram with Addition of Cards) diagram. [Found in CARL's UnCover database.]

Loney, Tim, and Arnie Bellefontaine. "TQM Training: The Library Service Challenge." *Journal of Library Administration* 18, no. 1/2 (1993):85-95.
Deals with the issue of training for TQM initiatives. Suggests four-phased training program.

Lowell, Gerald R., and Maureen Sullivan. "Self-Management in Technical Services: The Yale Experience." *Library Administration & Management* 4, no. 1 (Winter 1990):20-23.
Documents Yale's efforts in 1989 to reorganize its technical services department into self-regulating work groups consisting of: processing services, database management, preservation, and systems office. The article details the selection of the teams, team leaders, department heads, and special groups required for various parts of the implementation. Emphasizes need for complete training program.

Lynch, Richard, Lois Bacon, and Ted Barnes. "Creating Partnerships: Forging a Chain of Service Quality." *Journal of Library Administration* 18, no. 1/2 (1993):137-155.
Written by three individuals from the Faxon Company. Suggests libraries must seek partnerships to survive the future challenge of doing more with less. Provides Principles of Partnerships (p.142) that include the need for a TQM program in-house. Includes a sample partnership based on a technique called Service System Mapping.

*Mackey, Terry, and Kitty Mackey. "Think Quality! The Deming Approach *Does* Work in Libraries." *Library Journal* 117, no. 9 (May 15, 1992):57-61.
This article expounds upon one of the most renowned programs for total quality management—Deming's fourteen points. It focuses on many of the standard points, such as customer focus, importance of a mission statement, improvement of the process (not inspection of the product), and

includes various tools used in the structured TQM environment. Mackey and Mackey provide many good examples within each point to illustrate and support their premise. Management must take the initiative to make it happen in their organizations and "everyone in the organization must be willing to substitute teamwork for personal territory" (p.61) in order to acknowledge the importance of all service areas and to embrace true empowerment and cooperation. Training and retraining is critical. No bibliography is offered, but many titles are cited within the text.

Marshall, Mary. "Total Quality Management: A Selective Bibliography-Preliminary Version 1/15/92." *SLA Central Ohio Chapter Bulletin* 27, no. 2 (February 1992):6-7.
Contains basic titles from business and industry with three titles from library literature.

Martell, Charles, and John Tyson. "QWL Strategies: Quality Circles." *Journal of Academic Librarianship* 9, no. 5 (November 1983):285-287.
Martell and Tyson provide a brief but effective look at quality circles, their basic structure and approaches to implementation (including setting up a steering committee) and some ideas on library applications. The authors believe that quality circles are means by which library managers can positively and directly enhance employee morale and that commitment at the management level is crucial. Good, quick read.

Matysek, Eugene E. "Total Quality Management in the Defense Fuel Supply Center: Issues and Observations." *Journal of Library Administration* 18, no. 1/2 (1993):183-190.
Describes the TQM initiatives at the Defense Fuel Supply Center that were based on the criteria put forth by the Federal Quality Institute for the Quality Improvement Award.

McClure, Charles R., and Betsy Reifsnyder. "Performance Measures for Corporate Information Centers." *Special Libraries* 75, no. 3 (July 1984):193-204.
This is another article on library performance measures and one that provides a fairly thorough look, plus a bibliography. It uses the public library performance measures and applies them to the corporate information center. Most of the article consists of illustrations from *Output Measures for Public Libraries: A Manual of Standardized Procedures* (Chicago: ALA, 1982).

McGrath, William E. "The Reappearance of Rankings: Reliability, Validity, Explanation, Quality, and the Mission of Library and Information Science." *Library Quarterly* 63, no. 2 (April 1993):192-198.
Addresses the issue of quality in library and information science education. Considers students as customers until graduation when they become the product for employers to accept or reject. Has good references reflecting previous perspectives on quality in this area.

Mourey, Deborah A., and Jerry W. Mansfield. "Quality Circles for Management Decisions: What's in It for Libraries?" *Special Libraries* 75, no. 2 (April 1984):87-94.

This is one of the first, most extensive looks at the theory and practice of quality circles, one of the precursors to TQM teams. At the time of this article, quality circles were still fairly new in this country and much of the skepticism we see today was alive and well nine years ago. The advice early on in this article stays with you throughout the article and remains true today: "Take from quality circles what fits, works, and contributes to positive results and discard the rest. The long-term benefit of a better-trained, more skilled and confident employee is the greatest payoff" (p.88). The article goes on to define quality circles, a brief history of their application to that point in business and industry, how to establish a quality circle, the importance of training and management support, and 11 major benefits identified by Lockheed employees, a list worth looking at. It notes the application in particular at Duluth Public Library, a library that has been using quality circles since 1981, with training beginning as early as 1978. A good article.

Norton, Bob and Debbie Ellis. "Implementing BS 5750." *Aslib Information* 21, no. 6 (June 1993):242-245.

From a supportive stance, provides guidance on understanding BS 5750, and other applicable standards in the accreditation process. Offers a step-by-step guide through its various criteria, seeks to make the path clearer for the libraries interested in BS 5750 accreditation, and provides answers to many of the quandaries faced by libraries in these initiatives. An excellent offering for what appears to be a complex undertaking.

Norton, Bob, and Malcolm Peel. "Management and Managing." *Aslib Information* 20, no. 3 (March 1992):102-103.

Unless you subscribe to this journal, procuring this article isn't necessarily worth the interlibrary loan cost. However, if you can get to it easily, it is a crisp definition of what a manager is today, as well as a quick glimpse at "the manager" of the not too recent past. Unfortunately, some are still managing in that old style, the "life at the top" approach. Good litmus to decide which camp you manage from.

O'Brien, Patrick M. "Quality Leadership for the 21st Century." *Public Libraries* 11, no. 1/2 (1989):27-34.

Drawn much from the Robert K. Greenleaf 1970 monograph, *The Servant as Leader* (Newton Center, Mass.: Robert K. Greenleaf Center), this article deals with leadership qualities needed for managers of the twenty-first century library. O'Brien sets the stage with a preview of the twenty-first century library. In particular, he envisions "librarians ... revered as professionals in the information age, free to work exclusively with users, free to serve" (p.29). He believes that the qualities we will see in these new age librarians are vision (shared and clear), trust (in themselves as well as in their colleagues), effective listening, empowerment and sharing (co-owners of the vision), and tolerance (belief that all share the same vision but not all are equal in their capacity to serve).

Ojala, Marydee. "The Essence of Quality for Information Companies." *Information World Review* 82 (June 1993):18-19.
Discusses the status of quality initiatives in business today. Provides ideas on assuring quality of service to our information seekers by doing quality audits of our literature searches and by partnering with our database vendors (by proactively making suggestions for improvements) to improve the quality of the electronic information systems we and our users employ. Interesting section on complaints and the newer methods of registering them with vendors.

——. "Quality Online and Online Quality." *Online* 16, no. 1 (January 1992):73-75.
Basic thrust of article is to give online searchers advice on providing information on quality initiatives or in support of them. Includes a fairly recent study of the quality literature using Dialog's ABI/Inform and Management Contents. Also includes a brief overview of the Malcolm Baldrige National Quality Award and some of its winners.

O'Neil, Rosanna M., Richard L. Harwood, and Bonnie A. Osif. "A Total Look at Total Quality Management: A TQM Perspective from the Literature of Business, Industry, Higher Education, and Librarianship." *Library Administration & Management* 7, no. 4 (Fall 1993):244-254.
As the subtitle indicates, this article brings together the major quality literature to provide a comprehensive view for those who would like to get started along the quality trail. Includes the List for the Weary Manager, which provides a few titles as a backdrop to the TQM literature for those who have little time to plow through it all. Extensive references tied to the literary overview.

——. "A TQM Perspective: The Busy Manager's Bookshelf." *Library Administration & Management* 8, no. 1 (Winter 1994):49-52.
Following the above cited article, this is the first in the "Busy Manager's Bookshelf" column that will appear quarterly in *Library Administration & Management*. Its intent is to meet the needs of the busy manager by keeping abreast of current offerings for the new leaders of today who need time to lead and don't necessarily have time to read.

Paul, Meg. "Improving Service Provision." *The Australian Library Journal* 39, no. 1 (February 1990):64-69.
Focused on the word *service*, she believes "the sole purpose of libraries and librarianship is to service the library users by directing them to, or supplying them with the information and materials" (p.164). Borrowing from the private sector, she posits that a "philosophy of aims" is required from which good service will follow and discusses 12 such aims. She goes on to provide suggestions for a quality library environment. An article worth reading and sharing with your staff and colleagues.

Pearson, Christine M. "Aligning TQM and Organizational Learning." *Special Libraries* 84, no. 3 (Summer 1993):147-150.
Explores three topics: 1) why managers and executives currently find themselves faced with an array of "programs of the week"; 2) the fit between one such program, TQM, and organizational learning; and 3) potential misuses inherent in TQM.

Penniman, W. David. "Quality Reward and Awards: Quality Has Its Own Reward, But an Award Helps Speed the Process." *Journal of Library Administration* 18, no. 1/2 (1993)127-136.
Argues for creating a library quality award based upon the Malcolm Baldrige National Quality Award.

——. "Shaping the Future: The Council on Library Resources Helps to Fund Change." *Library Journal* 117, no. 7 (October 15, 1992):40-44.
Outlines the forces acting upon libraries today and how change is a must. Sees the challenges before us to become learning organizations. We must be able to prove our value to the information infrastructure to become the visionaries who meet the future.

Petrucciani, Alberto, and Igino Poggiali. "La Qualità Totale in Biblioteca" ["Total Quality in Libraries"]. *Bollettino AIB* 32, 1 (March 1992):7-20; 21-23. [In Italian, with an English summary.]
Addresses the general principles of TQM, and how they might be applied in Italian libraries and libraries in general, and uses "total quality" (TQ) and "company-wide quality control" (CWQC) as the jargon of choice. In one section, the authors take you through the various steps of a user getting a closed-stack item, illustrating how, in a multi-step process, we may think that just because they have the item they are satisfied. Whereas, they believe that at every step there could be wasted time or discourtesy, and although they may leave with what they came for, they may indeed leave dissatisfied. We need to change our assumptions of what service really is. This article is quite good with many worthwhile ideas, but it is unfortunately in Italian and the English translation is quite brief. Deserves to be fully translated into English.

Pluse, John. "Customer Focus: The Salvation of Service Organisations." *Public Library Journal* 6 (January/February 1990):1-5.

Porter, Lydia. "Quality Assurance: Going Round in Circles." *Aslib Information* 20, 6 (June 1992):240-241.
Defines quality assurance and focuses on four common tenets in the QA cycle to establish a model for library application. Good, practical, albeit brief, information concisely presented.

——. "Quality Initiatives in British Library and Information Services." *BLR&D Report 6105*. London: British Library, 1992.

Posnett, N. W. "Introduction of Performance Indicators at the Institute of Development Studies." *Journal of Information Science* 19, no. 5 (1993):377-387.

Documents the implementation of performance indicators at the Information Resource Unit of the Institute of Development Studies at the University of Sussex in Brighton. This is one of several performance indicators and measurement articles available, most of which have appeared in U.K. library and information science literature. The bibliography is quite good and more current than Blagden's *How Good Is Your Library?* but the latter's is more extensive and diverse.

Pybus, Ron. "Improvement of Services to Our Customers—The Modern Approach." *Public Library Journal* 7, no. 2. (March/April 1992):53-56.

Discusses the need to implement a library charter [in England]—"a ten commandments of what the customer is entitled to and can reasonably expect within a reasonable budget" (p.53). The charter would be based on the Citizens' Charter, which was put into law to establish standards of service for the "citizen," but that does not address libraries in particular. The library's charter should outline standards of service for areas such as registering and handling complaints, queuing time, compensation for poor service, telephone services, and empowerment of library personnel. While this article does not address TQM directly, it's the focus on the patron as customer that makes its a worthwhile article.

Quality Assurance in Libraries: The Health Care Sector. London: Library Association, 1990. (*See* Taylor, Margaret Haines.)

Quality Improvement Programs in ARL Libraries. Compiled by Jack Siggins and Maureen Sullivan. Washington, D.C.: Association of Research Libraries, Office of Management Services, 1993. (ARL SPEC Kit Series No. 196.)

Based on responses to an April 1993 survey of ARL libraries, this recent addition to the ARL SPEC Kit series, is a compilation of actual approaches to total quality application in 10 ARL libraries. The specimens include training outlines, team lists, graphs, definitions, references, and various internal memos. ARL/OMS also offers a "Draft Model for Adapting Total Quality Management in a Research Library," as well as their workshop outlines from Harvard and Michigan training sessions. A bountiful book of ideas, although it is much to weed through, as are others in this series.

Raven, Debby. "Quality Service in Beds." *Library Association Record* 93, no. 11 (November 1991):715.

This is included here so you won't waste time, curiosity, or money on it. Of interest to some, this is just a brief news item from Bedsfordshire, England, announcing the selection of the coordinator of their QA System.

Richards, David J. "Demonstrtating [*sic*] Excellence and the Value of Information Services." *Achieving Excellence: Proceedings of the 4th Asian Pacific Special and Law Librarians Conferences . . .*, 477-484. Canberra, Australia: Special Libraries and Health Libraries Sections, ALIA, and Australian Law Librarians Group, 1991.
Results of a research study titled "Identifying the Value of Library-based Information Services." This paper evaluates organizational excellence based on the model of quality, value, and benefit. A detailed evaluation of each aspect is provided. Within the quality section, quality management is defined and the application of TQM tools discussed and exemplified.

Riggs, Donald E. "Humanizing Library Management." *Library Administration & Management* 4, no. 1 (Winter 1990):7-8. [Introductory essay for 1990 Annual Theme: LA&M—Humanistic Management .]
Basically, "the days of the autocratic boss are fading" (p.7). Emphasizes the importance of respecting people, and of developing and nurturing staff potential through investment in training. The leader/manager of tomorrow must be compassionate and give greater attention to library-wide values in order to be an effective manager of the 1990s and beyond.

——. "Managing Quality: TQM in Libraries." *Library Administration & Management* 7, no. 2 (Spring 1992):73-78.
Provides a good, general overview of implementing TQM in the library setting, including some detail on his perspectives on training, identifying and selecting areas to study, teams, and the evaluation process. Riggs believes that all processes should be scrutinized for possible improvement. He also believes that training isn't necessary for all staff during the initial stages of TQM implementation. A good article.

*——. "Strategic Quality Management in Libraries." *Advances in Librarianship* 16 (1992):93-105.
An extensive contribution on this topic, it thoroughly represents a systems approach to quality. It first addresses the preliminary steps toward TQM: establishing the library's vision, mission, goals, and objectives. Riggs then takes the reader through the program strategies—strategies necessary for the realization of goals and objectives— the part of the process that is critical to the success of TQM and strategic planning. He suggests strategies such as personnel, innovation, and retrenchment, and then provides a gauge by which to judge their effectiveness. Next, Riggs walks through the implementation of TQM principles. He starts with an overview of the prominent figures in TQM theory (i.e., Juran, Crosby, and Deming) and includes their major principles and steps to quality improvement. While these three TQM gurus differ somewhat in their approaches, their generally accepted principles are provided by Riggs in a thorough description; they constitute the last seven pages of the chapter. One other item of note is the use here of yet another abbreviation in the area of quality assurance: SQM (strategic quality management), the combining of strategic planning and TQM. Riggs considers this union critical to the success of TQM in libraries for it ensures participation of the entire library.

*——. "TQM: Quality Improvement in New Clothes." Guest Editorial. *College & Research Libraries* 53, no. 6 (November 1992):481-482.
Though brief, this editorial provides a nice overview of TQM and its potential for library application. Here Riggs states that "TQM requires that the library's top management by work and deed, display commitment to continuous quality improvement" (p.481). He also points out four areas where libraries can benefit: 1) managing by fact, 2) eliminating rework, 3) respecting people and ideas, and 4) empowering people. He recommends against quick fixes and predicts a two- to three-year timeframe for proper staff preparation.

Rux, Paul. "TQM for Libraries." *Book Report* 11, no. 1 (January/February 1993):39.
A one-page theoretical look at the topic that includes a documented experience at a middle-school in Wisconsin. Doesn't add significantly to the literature, but perhaps the dissertation he's writing will.

Schroeder, Janet K. "Quality Circles: Rx for Ailing Libraries." *Technicalities* 3, no. 6 (June 1983):11-12.
This is one of the earliest applications of quality circles documented in our literature and reflects the work of the staff at the Duluth Public Library in Minnesota. Schroeder describes a "circle" as the level of commitment needed from library administration in order to pre-prepare to start using them, the components of teams, whether it's worth the effort, and how the staff and library benefits from the process. Schroeder also offers the results of a survey that asked the staff how they liked QCs. Good reading.

Scott, Colin. "Customer Care . . . or Customer Neglect." *Assistant Librarian* (1990):68-72.

Segal, JoAn S., and Tamiye Trejo-Meehan. "Quality Circles: Some Theory and Two Experiences." *Library Administration & Management* 4, no. 1 (Winter 1990):16-19.
Documents experiences in quality circle application at the Association of College and Research Libraries and the Chicago Public Library, with a brief introduction to quality circles through that period. The major contributions this article makes are the success and failure of quality circles based on environmental and personality factors, as well as a nice table that compares committees, task forces, and quality circles.

*Sell, Daniel, and Mary Ellen Mortola. "Quality Circles and Library Management." *Community & Junior College Libraries* 3, no. 3 (Spring 1985):[79]-92.
This article, similar to the Mourey and Mansfield article previously cited, gives an overview of the development of quality circles, from General Douglas McArthur to Quality Month. It defines quality circles, the philosophy, characteristics, and objectives. In particular, the authors provide a list of goals and objectives for making quality circles a successful management tool. It also details the creation of QCs, their implementation, and the various standard techniques. It includes an extensive bibliography.

Shaughnessy, Thomas W. "Benchmarking, Total Quality Management, and Libraries." *Library Administration & Management* 7, no.1 (Winter 1993):7-12.

One of the first articles to address the issue of benchmarking in libraries. Begins with a brief discussion of TQM in the academic setting and lists the essential components of TQM, zeroing in on one aspect: "the identification, collection, and the use of reliable data" (p.8). Libraries, he believes, will have difficulty in data collection due to the habitual lack of good data in many libraries that, he notes, has always been needed for effective strategic planning and decision making. Shaughnessy defines and lists the benefits of benchmarking and concludes that we may have to initially benchmark internally due to the lack of libraries to benchmark against. He provides a description of several benchmarking techniques. [Author's note: Shaughnessy concentrates on the user of the library as customer. We must not forget that in the TQM environment, internal customers are also important and, given the difficulty in gathering data on true user satisfaction, we may need to start with our internal processes to get some practice with TQM application while we try to figure out how we'll gather data from our external customers.]

———. "The Search for Quality." *Journal of Library Administration* 8, no. 1 (Spring 1987):5-10.

Addresses achieving and measuring quality in libraries. Offers 10 factors by which a library can determine the quality of its services including: reliability or consistency, responsiveness or timeliness, and understanding of customer needs, to name a few. Emphasizes total library commitment to service quality.

Sirkin, Arlene Farber. "Customer Service: Another Side of TQM." *Journal of Library Administration* 18, no. 1/2 (1993):71-83.

Discusses the customer focus of TQM, how to deal with this concept in libraries, and how to truly assess customer needs. Suggests a "strategic focus on customer service" (p.80) and provides some guidelines for getting there. Recommended reading.

Smith, Alan. "Are We at the Mercy of Quality?" *Aslib Information* 21, no. 6 (June 1993):240-241.

Warns against too much standardization in the quality process. Uses the BS 5750 approach, which is considered a method of assuring consistency that can include poor quality but at least consistent poor quality. Considers TQM different in that it is more a culture or a philosophy than a specific standard.

*Speakman, Gina. "Why Not Consider Quality Circles?" *Library Management* 12, no. 3 (1991):22-27.

Covers the basic characteristics and tenets of QCs, such as commitment and training. Speakman notes that the Japanese term for QCs when translated is " 'the gathering of the wisdom of the people' " (p.23), and she illustrates how this gathering of people helped to address the quality needs of three different libraries in England. She discusses the use of QCs in organizations from the perspective of advantages, criteria, and basic factors for success.

Spiegelman, Barbara M. "Total Quality Management in Libraries." *Library Management Quarterly* 16, no. 3 (Summer 1992):12-16.

Based on her experiences at Westinghouse, a long-time practitioner of TQM principles and philosophies, Spiegelman offers a different approach to applying TQM principles to library services. She uses the four imperatives (customer orientation, human resource excellence, product/process leadership, and management leadership) of Westinghouse's 12 Conditions of Excellence (later adapted as the seven criteria of the Baldrige award), and provides a list of questions under each (and its subcriteria) that the library should consider on the road to total quality. The answers to the questions are the beginnings of a TQM program. Excellent, practical information.

St. Clair, Gloriana. "Improving Quality: Organizational Benefits of Total Quality Management." Editorial in *College & Research Libraries* 54, no. 5 (September 1993):371-373.

One of several editorials written so far on TQM, St. Clair addresses how TQM causes a new way of thinking and addresses specific experiences at Penn State in team initiatives (i.e., self-directed work teams) and enhanced customer focus.

St. Clair, Guy. *Benchmarking, Total Quality Management and the Learning Organization: New Management Paradigms for the Information Environment—Introduction. Special Libraries* 84, no. 3 (Summer 1993):120-122.

Introduction to the special theme of this issue.

——. "The Future Challenge: Management and Measurement." *Special Libraries* 84, no. 3 (Summer 1993):151-154.

Discusses the measurement of one's successes in quality initiatives. The challenge library managers face is two-fold: our ability to measure, in terms that meet the needs of management, our value within the organization; and to gain acceptance of senior management for the value of our contributions to the organization.

Stone, Jason R. "Quality Circles in the Library." *New Jersey Libraries* 20 (Summer 1987):13-19.

The East Brunswick Public Library established its first quality circle in the fall of 1984 to study overcrowding at peak hours. They established a quality circle coordinator position as the individual who coordinated in-house training, a member manual, a newsletter, and so on, documenting QC progress. This individual also served as facilitator and maintained records of the meetings. Membership on the team was voluntary, a code of conduct for the team was established and added to the manual, meetings were kept to one hour and were not scheduled at times that would compromise public service or other daily operations. Details of the study are provided.

Stuart, Chit, and Miriam Drake. "TQM in Research Libraries." *Special Libraries* 84, no. 3 (Summer 1993):131-136.

Highlights reasons for initial failures of TQM efforts in industry and bases the rest of the article on TQM application at the Georgia Institute of Technology. According to Stuart and Drake, customer-orientation seems to have eluded libraries for "librarians often failed to realize that the library is not the information source of choice for many faculty and students. Librarians were more concerned with internal process rather than perceptions of value or customer service. They saw themselves as keepers of knowledge rather than active agents in information transfer" (p.132).

Sullivan, Maureen, and Jack A. Siggins. "Total Quality Management Initiatives in Higher Education." *Journal of Library Administration* 18, no. 1/2 (1993):157-170.

Provides an overview of TQM applications in higher education and the catalysts for this change.

Taylor, Margaret Haines. *QA: Quality Assurance in Libraries.* Ottawa: Canadian Library Association, 1990. [Also published under the title *Quality Assurance in Libraries: The Health Care Sector.* London: Library Association, 1990.]

Based on practical applications of quality assurance principles in health care/medical libraries in both Canada and the United Kingdom, this monograph assists in bridging the gap for libraries in search of actual QA applications in special libraries. Includes chapters on database search services, consumer health education, standards-setting in Canada and the United Kingdom, interlibrary loan standards, and collection evaluation. Highly recommended for any type of library is the "Strategic Planning" chapter (p. 1-15). The latter includes concise definitions of mission, goals, objectives, and action plans. Noticeably absent, however, is the definition and use of the term "vision."

Teeter, Deborah J., and G. Gregory Lozier. "Pursuit of Quality in Higher Education: Case Studies in Total Quality Management." *New Directions for Institutional Research* no. 78 (Summer 1993). San Francisco: Jossey-Bass Publishers, 1993.

While this volume represents only a minute reference to what is going on in libraries involved in TQM initiatives (Samford University has a chapter and small paragraph), this volume is included because it features invaluable appendices of the levels of involvement and progress of 15 institutions of higher education of varying sizes that may prove useful for some libraries for benchmarking purposes.

Tenopir, Carol. "Database Quality Revisited." *Library Journal* 115, no. 16 (October 1, 1990):64-67.

———. "Quality Control." *Library Journal* 112, no. 3 (February 15, 1987):124-125.

In 1987, Tenopir noted the surge of quality control as a major concern for database users. She prescribed several quality factors and discussed each at length. In 1990, she revisits the database quality issue to note its resurgence as the hot topic she long expected and highlights the many critical developments. In particular, the proposed SCOUG (Southern California Online Users Group) rating scheme is featured.

Tomlin, Anne C. "Quality Improvement and Health Care: An Annotated Bibliography." *Medical Reference Services Quarterly* 11, no. 2 (Summer 1992):13-26.

Tomlin explains first why the health care industry is moving in the continuous quality improvement (CQI) direction. She notes the sparseness of information on the application of this process in libraries and seeks to provide a resource for those who would like to know more about CQI, in the health care industry in particular. Includes 28 annotated entries from the medical field using MEDLINE and Health Planning and Administration from 1988 to the present.

"Total Quality Management in the One-Person Library: A Further Look." *The One-Person Library* 9, no. 6 (October 1992).

"TQM in the OPL." *The One-Person Library* 9, no. 5 (September 1992):1-3.

The two articles provide TQM ideas to the one-person library (OPL) regardless of the level of institutional commitment or interest. According to the September issue, of the essential ingredients of TQM, three are appropriate to the OPL regardless of library type: focus on customer satisfaction, fact-based measurement, and commitment to continuous improvement of products and services. The author also believes that the OPL can be part of a team by partnering with those with whom they work in the larger organization everyday. May not be a true TQM process, but teamwork and trust are nonetheless an option. In the sequel, the author recommends, as another method of TQM participation for the OPL, to take a leadership role in the organization in making TQM happen. By setting up a program and then sharing that program with the manager, the OPL can be the catalyst for change. Suggests various means of getting training outside the organizational boundaries.

Towler, Constance F. "Problem Solving Teams in Total Quality Management." *Journal of Library Administration* 18, no. 1/2 (1993):97-112.

Addresses the team aspect of TQM: forming, facilitating, record keeping, and problem solving. Also suggests training program for team problem solving.

Usherwood, Bob. "Managing Public Libraries as a Public Service." *Public Library Journal* 7, no. 6 (November/December 1992):141-145.

Using terms such as "marketingspeak" and "loadsamoney," Usherwood questions the veracity of applying private sector management principles to the public sector where the missions and economies of scale differ. Geared primarily toward libraries in the United Kingdom, it offers much to consider for all types of libraries wherever they are. And if you like to collect library-related quotes, especially for public speaking engagements, this article is filled with them. Despite the political innuendos (which this U.S. librarian had a difficult time relating to), this is an interesting article. (*Cf.* Carl Clayton's response to Usherwood in "Quality and the Public Services.")

Walton, Mary. *Deming at Work.* New York: Perigee Books (Putnam), 1991.

This monograph documents case studies of the application of Deming's principles in various companies. The work recounts the success stories of two of the corporate libraries, the Happy Bookers and the Clippers, of the Florida Power and Light Company (the latter being a prime TQM success story unto itself because it was the first company outside of Japan to win the Deming Prize).

Warnken, Paula. "What is Total Quality Management and What Is It Doing in My Library?" Part 1 and 2. *The Unabashed Librarian* no. 85 (1992):9-10; no. 86 (1992):7-8.

Part 1 provides a short, basic overview of TQM. It Includes five basic elements with some discussion of each. No bibliography, but a nice synopsis to share with the uninformed. Part 2 documents a quality approach they took titled Improved Library Service for which they established five goals. It appears that they began implementing a TQM-based program without realizing it and Warnken describes the parallels. Recommended.

Wedlake, Linda J. "An Introduction to Quality Assurance and a Guide to the Implementation of BS 5750." *Aslib Proceedings* 45, no. 1 (January 1993):23-30.

Extensive look at the quality system environment in light of the quality assurance philosophy and the development of the British Standard for Quality Systems and BS 5750. Article includes guidance on manuals and procedures, a guide to implementation of BS 5750, and how to audit one's quality system.

*Whitehall, Tom. "Quality in Library and Information Service: A Review." *Library Management* 13, no. 5 (1992):23-35.

Provides an extensive overview of not only the quality of information, but the quality of service in libraries. Includes an extensive citation list (90 entries).

Whitlach, Jo Bell. "Unobtrusive Studies and the Quality of Academic Library Reference Services." *College & Research Libraries* 50, no. 2 (March 1989):181-194.

Discusses the differences between obtrusive and unobtrusive studies and the assumptions underlying the latter methodology. Whitlach, at that time, had just completed an obtrusive study of reference performances and believes her findings indicate that the manner in which unobtrusive studies are currently conducted are very limited in their ability to judge reference services quality, and obtrusive studies have their shortcomings as well. Whitlach concludes her article with recommendations for improving reference evaluation.

Willis, Alfred, and Eugene E. Matysek. "Place and Functionality of Reference Services from the Perspective of Quality Management Theory." *Library and Information Science Research Electronic Conference 2.8 Feature Article.* (August 20, 1992):320 lines.
   Very interesting contribution to overall quality management in libraries on the "processes" of libraries, how they interrelate, and how it is the "number of ... patrons [requesting assistance] that is the index of a library's processual inefficiency" (line 271). Basically, the premise is that "any process can be described as a series of events progressively moving forward over time to produce products or services for a customer" (line 38) and that "much if not all reference service actually functions as a corrective for occasional processual inefficiencies" (line 72). Describes the "optimally functioning library" and how it provides "information packets" to its customers. The comments that follow this controversial and intriguing perception of the intricacies of library services are equally intriguing.

Winkworth, Ian. "Performance Indicators and Quality Assurance." *Aslib Information* 21, no. 6 (June 1993):250-251.
   Suggests performance indicators as a methodology (in the realm of TQM) for setting standards of quality and then measuring against them for continuous improvement.

Young, Vicki. "Focus on Focus Groups." *College & Research Library News* 54, no. 7 (July/August 1993):391-394.
   Outlines one of the tools steps to running focus groups and includes a good, select bibliography for further research.

Younger, Jennifer. "Total Quality Management: Can We Move Beyond the Jargon?" *ALCTS Newsletter* 2, no. 8 (1991):81-83.
   This thought piece provides a general theoretical overview, and emphasizes some of the basic points of TQM: customer as focus; the Deming theory that 94 percent of the problems in quality are with the process, only 6 percent with the people; and the necessity for the entire organization to be on board in order to have a successful cultural change. Younger contends that TQM should not be just a trend, but rather that we as managers should explore its potential in libraries.

Appendix A:
Creating an In-House
Support Collection

The following list of titles is provided to assist you in building an in-house collection to support the quality efforts of you and your staff. Such a collection may or may not be necessary depending upon how involved the rest of your institution is and its potential drain on your collections. I found that some materials were just not available and that putting them in our libraries' noncirculating reference collections made it difficult for our staff members to take the materials home (not to mention being able to use them in their meetings). We currently have about 20 titles in our collection and are still collecting, always being sure to have one copy in the general collection as well.

TQM is not just working methodically through a process, it is a multifaceted process that requires teamwork and good leadership skills. The collection recommended below includes titles that support these two aspects and offer practical support for the "quality tools," which when newly introduced can be particularly confusing.

For each title a full citation is provided, as well as ISBN and price from *BIP Plus* (if the title is a U.S. imprint) as of January 1994 or directly from the publisher. The list below is select, so it isn't too expensive to get started. No articles are noted, but as good articles are found I suggest a binder or vertical file be started to encourage growth and up-to-date readings.

The literature in this area is exploding. Keeping the in-house collection stocked with only the essentials should work well for your program. Once you embark on this journey and have put to use its principles and processes, you will find it is no longer a program, but a way of life and the tools will become second nature. Training for new employees will continue to make this in-house collection of value.

Suggested In-House Collection

Brassard, Michael, ed. and comp. *The Memory Jogger™: A Pocket Guide of Tools for Continuous Improvement*. 2d ed. Methuen, Mass.: GOAL/QPC, 1988. $4.25. ISBN 1-879364-03-4.

This publisher offers truly fine material for TQM initiatives. This is a concise and inexpensive guide for the practical application of quality tools; a small (13 cm.) and handy tool that every team should have at its fingertips if the TQM program you're following doesn't provide one of its own. (Dupont, for example, has put together its own tool book for its in-house quality efforts.)

————. *The Memory Jogger Plus+*[TM]*: Featuring the Seven Management and Planning Tools.* Methuen, Mass.: GOAL/QPC, 1989. $29.95. ISBN 1-87936-402-6.

An expanded version of *The Memory Jogger*, this is an extensive support tool for applying the tools of total quality management. Includes pocket cards that illustrate the seven tools. If the organization you work for has its own set of tools, this text can serve to supplement them.

Camp, Robert C. *Benchmarking: The Search for Industry Best Practices That Lead to Superior Performance.* Milwaukee, Wis.: ASQC Quality Press, 1989. $34.95. ISBN 0-87389-058-2.

This manual appears in almost every article you read about benchmarking, most likely because it provides superior guidance on benchmarking the topic.

Douglass, Merrill E., and Donna N. Douglass. *Time Management for Teams.* New York: AMACOM, 1992. $17.95. ISBN 0-8144-7804-2.

Offers advice on such team concerns as effective presentation skills, improving communication, evaluative checklists, surveys, and instructions on how to deal with the four "team temperaments."

Doyle, Michael, and David Straus. *How to Make Meetings Work: The New Interactive Method.* New York: Jove Publications, 1986. $4.99. ISBN 0-515-09048-4.

An inexpensive paperback documenting what the authors call "the interaction method." If their tools and techniques are followed, meetings become more effective and productive. They assist in deciding whether or not to have a meeting at all, and provide solutions for 16 types of problem people. With meetings being a necessary element in TQM, and the TQM process a somewhat long one, the smoother the meeting process, including effective post-meeting follow through, the better chance your TQM efforts have of succeeding. If anything, I recommend this tool for running better meetings.

Fournies, Ferdinand F. *Coaching for Improved Work Performance.* Blue Ridge Summit, Pa.: Liberty Hall Books, 1987. $12.95. ISBN 0-8306-3054-6.

"The single purpose of this book is to help managers do better what they get paid to do, to improve their subordinates' performances, quantitatively and qualitatively, through specific, face-to-face techniques called coaching" (p. ix). While TQM itself is the change agent for most in this new culture, the road to the new culture requires a leader who is constantly coaching the staff through the ups and downs of this process.

Gilbert, John. *How to Eat an Elephant: A Slice by Slice Guide to Total Quality Management.* Merseyside, England: Tudor Business Publishing, 1992. £14.95. ISBN 1-872807-80-1.

"This book has been written with the purpose of getting some fun from Total Quality Management (TQM), a continuous process of change made as dry as loft fluff by most of the people who write about it and teach it.... There isn't much structure to this book; you can open it anywhere, have a thought provoking read or a chuckle and shut it again." This is an excellent, light-hearted work and is part of my personal collection on TQM.

Harrington-Mackin, Deborah. *The Team Building Tool Kit: Tips, Tactics, and Rules for Effective Workplace Teams.* New York: AMACOM, 1994. $17.95. ISBN 0-8144-7826-3.

Written by a management consultant with hands-on experience in team-building training and guidance, this monograph provides a step-by-step approach to creating self-directed work teams in the workplace, a critical, but overlooked aspect of TQM strategies. Noting a few chapters, this tool includes how to get started, setting up and running meetings, team behavior analysis, training, and rewards. Also includes in each chapter a Q&A section that addresses some of the common questions of management and staff regarding this approach to the workforce.

The Idea Book: Improvement Through TQI (Total Quality Improvement). [English translation of *Kaizen teian handobukku.*] Cambridge, Mass.: Productivity Press, 1988. $55.00. ISBN 0-915299-22-4.

Directed at workers as a practical tool with hundreds of examples and suggestions, this monograph is based on the Japanese approach of management commitment and involvement, timely response, and a reward system also known as "kaizen." Workers are quoted in the book about their experiences in putting forth suggestions and seeing them come to fruition.

Juran, J. M., and Frank M. Gyrna. *Juran's Quality Control Handbook.* 4th ed. New York: McGraw-Hill, 1988. $93.50. ISBN 0-07-033176-6 pa.

The complete reference tool for your collection. Nearly 1,500 pages in length, it includes assistance for such key TQM needs as problem resolution, thorough explanation of the quality tools, and review material for self-training and the training of others. It also serves as an excellent reference tool, review material for preparing for meetings, and fodder for authoritatively and convincingly selling the TQM idea to others. It has a great glossary; other terms are defined throughout the text [a shortfall because not all terms are in the glossary]; assistance in team building, implementing change, and making the transition from training to implementation; and the index is fifty pages long. Excellent.

Kelles, Michael R. *Everyone's Problem-Solving Handbook: Step-by-Step Solutions for Quality Improvement.* White Plains, N.Y.: Quality Resources, 1992. $18.50. ISBN 0-527-91652-8.

This ideal reference tool includes an excellent bibliography, glossary, and five case studies to help conceptualize the application of these quality tools. Introduces the idea of the "QI story" through which, in five simple steps, a team can present the fruits of its labor, mostly through illustration.

Resources for the Implementation of Total Quality Management (TQM): In Education, in Nonprofits, and in the Service Sector. Compiled by Anne Blankenbaker. Edited by Maureen Sullivan. Washington, D.C.: Office of Management Services, Association of Research Libraries, 1992. $7.50 for ARL members; $10.00 for non-members.

An annotated bibliography that addresses significant works in the areas noted in the title, and provides a journal for monitoring and associations to contact.

Scholtes, Peter R. *The Team Handbook: How to Use Teams to Improve Quality.* Madison, Wis.: Joiner Associates, 1988. $39.00. ISBN 0-9622264-0-8.

If teams don't function effectively, the TQM process doesn't work. Scholtes' book is considered one of the best on the market and if you can only purchase one of the team-oriented books in this appendix, I would suggest this one. If you want to run your own training program, Joiner Associates also offers the *Team Companion,* which consists of 250 transparencies, handbooks, guide cards, posters, and so on, that facilitates the teaching of these principles. ($550.00 including a canvas carry-all. For $450.00 you can purchase the set without carry-all and posters.)

Scott, Cynthia D., and Dennis T. Jaffe. *Managing Organizational Change: A Practical Guide for Managers.* Menlo Park, Calif.: Crisp Publications, 1989. $8.95. ISBN 0-931961-80-7.

This guide is meant to assist managers in maintaining performance under the chaotic conditions brought on by organizational change. Using the guide can make an effective "change leader" out of you. It also includes a video (which I have not viewed). However, a free catalog of all the offerings can be ordered by writing to Crisp Publications, Inc., 1200 Hamilton Court, Menlo Park, California, 94025, or calling (415) 323-6100.

Sibbet, David., Allan Drexler, and the team at The Grove Consultants International. *Graphic Guide to Best Team Practices.* Version 2.0. San Francisco: The Grove Consultants International, 1993. $59.00. ISBN 1-879502-01-1.

A book loaded with ideas for team leaders, this guide offers a full program for starting up your teams and keeping them invigorated. The authors believe that the "best tools are simple and flexible" (p.1) ones and the majority of this spiral-bound work consists of one-page "practices." Each page has a title (e.g., Small Wins), notes the place in the team work strategy (e.g., implementation), time one should spend on this activity (e.g., 1-3 hours), a key phrase (e.g., Succeed a Step-at-a-Time), tips, steps of the process, and illustrations appropriate to the activity. The info-bites are very useful, although the desk-top, digitized images of real people are a bit out of the ordinary. It also includes the application of various quality tools such as the Gantt chart and Pareto analysis.

Zenger, John H., Ed Musselwhite, Kathleen Hurson, and Craig Perrin. *Leading Teams: Mastering the New Role*. Homewood, Ill.: Business One Irwin, 1994. $30.00. ISBN 1-55623-894-0.

Written by a consulting firm specializing in team leadership consulting (there's a large manual for those who subscribe to the firm's services), this title focuses on the leader aspect of teams and provides step-by-step, as well as situational instructions, on how to be an expert leader. A strong team leader is an essential element of optimal team performance.

Other Titles to Consider for the Circulation Collection

The following titles are suggested for your general collection if your library lacks sufficient funds to purchase them for both the circulating collection and your staff support collection.

Campbell, Andrew, and Laura L. Nash. *A Sense of Mission: Defining Direction for the Large Corporation*. Reading, Mass.: Addison-Wesley, 1992. $28.95. ISBN 0-201-60800-6.

This book is meant to guide you in the creation of a mission statement and to make that statement become a reality for your organization. The mission is the critical first step for customer service and strategic planning and this book makes the creation of this statement much easier.

Covey, Stephen R. *Principle-Centered Leadership*. New York: Fireside, 1992. $12.00. ISBN 0-671-79280-6.

Author of *The Seven Habits of Highly Effective People*, Covey believes that trust in an organization is critical to an organization's success. To be trusted, leaders must base their actions on sound, universally accepted principles. This book also includes chapters on total quality management and how principle-centered leadership folds into that philosophy and practice.

Senge, Peter. *The Fifth Discipline: The Art and Practice of the Learning Organization*. New York: Doubleday Currency, 1990. $25.00. ISBN 0-385-26094-6.

Although some think this book is a bit daunting, it is the major work on the learning organization concept and Senge is the guru on this topic. It's an approach to organizational theory, which must be taken a dose at a time, but it is definitely worth considering in an organization adopting TQM philosophies. The thrust of the learning organization is best summarized in Senge's words, "The tools and ideas presented in this book are for destroying the illusion that the world is created of separate, unrelated forces. When we give up this illusion—we can then build 'learning organizations,' organizations where people continually expand their capacity to create the results they truly desire, where new and expansive patterns of thinking are nurtured, where collective aspiration is set free, and where people are continually learning how to learn together" (p.4). It is composed of five component technologies (personal disciplines): systems thinking, personal mastery, mental models, building shared vision, and team learning with systems thinking being the fifth discipline that brings it all together.

The Source: A Total Quality Management Information Guide. 1992 ed., plus annual supplements. Methuen, Mass.: GOAL/QPC, 1992. $74.95. ISBN 1-879364-19-0.

Issued in a loose-leaf binder for adding supplemental updates, this is an extensive, annotated bibliography representing publications of all types (articles, books, proceedings) on total quality practices in business and industry. (The first supplement was almost as large as the original volume.) If your institution is involved in TQM, your library would benefit from this work.

Total Quality Management: Strategies for Local Government. Washington, D.C.: International City/County Management Association, 1993. 2 vols. $150.00.

This is a two-volume set consisting of the *Leader's Guide* and the *Participant's Handbook*. It is designed to be used for conducting a six-day workshop, including a suggested pre-workshop memo and questionnaire. The *Leader's Guide* includes the lesson plans for the workshop, lesson overview for the six days, guidelines for implementation (planning for the workshop and its activities), hints for conducting group sessions, tailoring the workshop, and guidelines for assessing the training needs of the organization. The *Participant's Handbook* is simply excellent and offers the following modules: awareness and history, an introduction, implementation timetables, a good bibliography, and a glossary, to name just a few. Although meant for a government-oriented audience, it is fairly generic and is an excellent basis for creating an in-house program, although the copyright is fairly restrictive.

Appendix B:
Getting Trained

Formal training in TQM can be a bit expensive unless you are fortunate enough to have it provided by your parent institution. The following organizations offer opportunities for training in TQM, both contractual and in-house. (Note: No particular one is recommended or ranked above the others.)

American Management Association
135 West 50th Street
New York, NY 10020
Tel: (800) 262-9699 (orders and catalogs)
A new offering from the self-study series of the AMA is *Total Quality Management*. According to a recent brochure, "it reviews the history of quality and examines the wide variety of philosophies, concepts, and techniques for managing, controlling, and improving quality. Finally, it takes you step-by-step through the implementation process." It costs $110.00, with a 10 percent discount for members. The AMA also offers a full range of total quality management seminars, as well as seminars for the peripheral skills such as communication, leadership, and so on.

Association of Research Libraries
Office of Management Services
21 Dupont Circle, NW, Suite 800
Washington, DC 20036
(202) 296-8656
Under the umbrella of *Leadership and Learning*, ARL offers a program titled "Implementing Continuous Improvement Programs." While I have not attended this particular one, the other ARL/OMS I have attended have been quite good.

Special Libraries Association
Professional Development Center
1700 Eighteenth Street, NW
Washington, DC 20009-2508
(202) 234-4700
In addition to the "Quality Imperative" workshop, others are offered as well. (For a review of the "Quality Imperative" workshop, see O'Neil, et al.'s "A TQM Perspective: The Busy Manager's Bookshelf" in *Library Administration & Management* 8, no. 1 [Winter 1994]:50.)

Joiner Associates, Inc.
3800 Regent Street
P.O. Box 5445
Madison, WI 53705-0445
(800) 669-8326
Produced in 1992, Joiner Associates put together *The Team Companion: Instructional Tools for the Team Handbook*. It includes transparencies, posters, guide cards, worksheets, handouts, and more. While I have neither used nor actually handled this item, *The Team Handbook*, upon which this is based, is excellent. If you don't have other training opportunities and can afford this training kit, it appears to be quite a complete training tool. The cost is $550.00 ($440.00 without posters or bag) for the package and it has a 30-day money-back guarantee.

International City/County Management Association
Distribution Center
P.O. Box 2011
Annapolis Junction, MD 20701-2011
(800) 745-8780
Total Quality Management: Strategies for Local Government. Washington, DC: International City/County Management Association, 1993. (2 vols., $150.00)
This is a two-volume set consisting of the *Leader's Guide* and the *Participant's Handbook*. It is designed to be used for conducting a six-day workshop, including a suggested pre-workshop memo and questionnaire. The *Leader's Guide* includes the lesson plans for the workshop, lesson overview for the six days, guidelines for implementation (planning for the workshop and its activities), hints for conducting group sessions, tailoring the workshop, and guidelines for assessing the training needs of the organization. The *Participant's Handbook* is simply excellent and offers the following modules: awareness and history, an introduction, implementation timetables, a good bibliography, and a glossary, to name just a few. Although meant for a government-oriented audience, it is fairly generic and is an excellent basis for creating an in-house program, although the copyright is fairly restrictive. A video titled *Quality: A Commitment to Continuous Improvement* is also available to borrow for 10 business days.

Other Options

Several other consulting and training firms around the country also offer total quality management seminars of varying lengths. The obvious first and best step is to investigate the offerings of your own organization to realize the best support for a quality program. Otherwise, be sure to select a reputable firm, one that most closely follows the Deming, Juran, or Crosby approach, and one that has a money-back guarantee!

Appendix C: The Electronic Information Highway

The electronic roads that have opened for accessing information on any topic can be truly mind-boggling, so I would be remiss if I didn't include some options and instructions for using this method of accessing information, opportunities, and so forth, on TQM.

Below I've listed existing Listservs to which you can subscribe. But if you have Gopher access, you can use its searching software (VERONICA in most places) to find sources of information on TQM worldwide (that's how I obtained instructions for joining two of the three Listservs below). Happy searching!

TQMLIB (Total Quality Management for Libraries):
To subscribe: Request information from Barton Lessing at
BLESSING@WAYNEST1.BITNET.

TQM-L (TQM in Higher Education):
To subscribe:
Send the following command to LISTSERV@ukanvm.bitnet, or
LISTSERV@ukanvm.cc.ukans.edu

SUBSCRIBE TQM-L Yourfirstname Yourlastname

QUALITY (TQM in Manufacturing & Service Industries):
To subscribe:
Send the following command to LISTSERV@PUCC.PRINCETON.BITNET, or
LISTSERV@PUCC.PRINCETON.EDU

SUBSCRIBE QUALITY Yourfirstname Yourlastname

Appendix D:
The Quality Awards

There is an excellent chapter on the quality awards, with discussions, in the first volume of *Advances in Total Quality Management* (see Appendix E). Below are listed some of the awards talked about in that chapter (marked with an *), as well as others of interest. Addresses for additional information on certain quality awards were not available.

The Deming Prize*
Secretariat of the Deming Prize Committee
Japanese Union of Scientists and Engineers
5-10-11 Sendagaya, Shibuya-Ku
Tokyo 151
Japan
The Japanese prize for total quality excellence established in 1951 by the Japanese Union of Scientists and Engineers.

European Quality Award*
European Foundation for Quality Management
Building "Reaal" Dellenoord 47A
5612 AA Endhove
Netherlands
Tel.: 31 40 461075; Fax: 31 40 432005
Presented for the first time in 1992, it is awarded by the members of the European Foundation for Quality Management to Western European businesses that best espouse the practices and philosophies of total quality based on the criteria of their award. They also offer special prizes for those who exhibit total quality initiatives.

Japan Quality Control Model
One step above the Deming Prize, this award is a medal sponsored by the Union of Japanese Scientists and Engineers with winners selected by the Deming Prize committee.

Malcolm Baldrige National Quality Award*
NIST
Rte. 270 and Quince Orchard Road
Administration Building, Room A537
Gaithersburg, MD 20899
USA
Tel.: (301) 975-2036; Fax: (301) 948-3716

Created by an act of Congress in 1987, this is the much sought after U.S. award for total quality excellence. Information can be obtained free of charge from the above address and it includes a comprehensive document outlining the application and criteria for the award. This document provides unparalleled guidance on defining quality in an organization and for quality auditing, whether or not an organization intends to apply for the award.

Pennsylvania Quality Leadership Awards
Pennsylvania Quality Leadership Foundation
MS 210/26
939 East Park Drive
Harrisburg, PA 17111-2810
USA
Tel. (717) 561-7100; Fax: (717) 561-7104

A result of the 1992 Pennsylvania Quality Improvement Act, the state of Pennsylvania recently created statewide awards with the goal of promoting quality initiatives across the state, including efforts in the academic, industrial, and government sectors. Other states and cities have also established awards, therefore, calling your government offices (including chambers of commerce) should prove fruitful.

Perkins Award
National Society for Quality Through Teamwork
2 Castle Street
Salisbury SP1 1BB
England

Established by Perkins Engines (Peterborough, England) in 1987 and coordinated by the National Society for Quality Through Teamwork, it aims to honor the company that maximizes employee involvement in its quality efforts.

Appendix E: Publications in Total Quality Management

Many good publications provide continuous learning opportunities in the area of total quality management (TQM). The following titles are worth monitoring; there are actually several more, but they primarily focus on manufacturing and so were excluded from this list.

Advances in Total Quality Management. Abingdon, Oxfordshire, England: Carfax.
   This is a series newly begun in 1993. It is a supplement to the journal *Total Quality Management*, also published by Carfax. Each volume is thematically titled. The first one in 1993 was titled "Total Quality Management Process: A Systematic Approach." The second volume's intended title is "The Quality Journey."

AQP Annual Conference and Resource Mart. Cincinnati, Ohio: Association for Quality and Participation.
   Each conference consists of papers addressing such aspects of total quality as team development, the Malcolm Baldrige award, customer service, employee involvement, human resources management, and so on. It is a gold mine of current TQM applications.

Aslib Information. London: Association for Information Management.

Aslib Proceedings. London: Association for Information Management.

Bulletin of the Medical Library Association. Chicago: Medical Library Association.

Journal for Quality and Participation. Cincinnati, Ohio: Association for Quality and Participation.

Library Administration & Management. Chicago: ALA/Library Administration and Management Association.

Library Management. Bradford, West Yorkshire, England: MCB University Press.

National Productivity Review. New York: Executive Enterprises.

Organizational Dynamics. New York: American Management Association.

Success. Chicago: Success Magazine.

Total Quality Management. Abingdon, Oxfordshire, England: Carfax.

Training. Minneapolis, Minn.: Lakewood Publications.

Glossary of Total Quality

This glossary will assist you in understanding the terms found in the reprinted articles and the annotated bibliography, as well as provide you with some of the other terminology found in the total quality area.

Because it is a relatively new field still, total quality management (TQM) and its associated terminology is widely interpreted, and therefore the definitions for some of the terminology listed in this glossary will certainly be subject to debate. The terms below were defined based upon their use in the total quality movement as initiated by Deming, Juran, Ishikawa, and Shewhart, as well as in the reprinted articles and annotated bibliography of this sourcebook. While this glossary does not contain every term associated with TQM, it is fairly extensive and should be a useful resource for your reference shelf.

affinity diagram. Gathers and organizes large amounts of data into groupings based on similarities and common relationships. It serves to expand the thinking around a large or complex issue.

baseline. The level of current performance used to compare with future performance to determine relative improvement. For example, current acquisition of domestic titles may take three months. When it is reduced, the measure of improvement is compared against this earlier time frame.

benchmarking. The continuous measuring of products, services, practices, and performance against the achievements of the best in that respective industry, and then striving to meet and surpass those standards. Can also involve comparing outside of one's industry, as well as basing the benchmarks on customer input. Also called **best practice benchmarking**.

best-in-class. An item or service that is superior to all other like products or services in terms of effectiveness, efficiency, adaptability, value, and customer-focus. *See also* **benchmarking**.

best practice benchmarking. *See* **benchmarking**.

brainstorming. A method for gathering the ideas of a group where all ideas are shared and may then be grouped and prioritized. It is useful in gaining the expertise of all in the group, and thus securing a maximum number of ideas for use in problem solving, innovation efforts, design activities, and so forth. A type of **nominal group technique**.

169

breakthrough. This is a term generally attributed to Dr. Joseph Juran that describes a significant quality improvement which results in a single, significant change in a process. It is a movement forward that is considered revolutionary.

BS 5750. British Standard, issued in multiple parts, based on the international standard ISO 9000.

cause. The proven reason or source of variation behind a situation, problem, or deficiency.

cause-and-effect diagram. Also known as the Fishbone or Ishikawa diagram, this is a graphical method for isolating a problem, or effect, and its causes. For example, an effect could be: There is an increase in stolen cars. The causes in the diagram answer the question: Why? The diagram also aids in determining the "root causes" of a problem, situation, or deficiency. Conceived by Kaoru Ishikawa.

check sheet. Gathers data based on sample observations. Answers the question: How often do certain things happen? Will accentuate underlying patterns.

common cause. The opposite of special causes, these are causes that are frequently and consistently causing errors in the process and that can be addressed for improvement. For example, the circulation system frequently goes off-line which causes lines at the circulation desk. Studied by using a **process performance chart**.

company-wide quality control (CWQC). Based on Feigenbaum's Total Quality Control principles, this is a strategic quality program that is company-wide. The Japanese application was different in that rather than having a QC specialist (as espoused by Feigenbaum) be responsible for ensuring quality, everyone is responsible for studying, practicing, participating, and promoting QC. It is this approach to total quality that caused the Japanese to coin this newer phrase (CWQC) in 1968, and is the approach most synonymous with total quality management. **Company-wide quality management** (CWQM) is also sometimes the terms used for this strategy.[1]

company-wide quality management (CWQM). *See* **company-wide quality control**.

consensus. Not to be confused with majority voting or unanimity, a team that meets consensus agrees that everyone in the group can live with the decision and will support it. A majority vote does not ensure consensus.

continuous quality improvement (CQI). One of the popular program labels for total quality management, continuous quality improvement is actually a fundamental element of TQM but the two are being used interchangeably. For some, using this phrase and eliminating the word "management" drives out some of the fear and skepticism.

continuous quality improvement team. *See* **quality circle**.

control. The method of regulating processes and systems by measuring actual performance, comparing it against standards, and acting on any differences.

control chart. *See* **process performance chart**.

corrective action team. *See* **quality circle**.

cost of poor quality. Costs that occur due to the poor quality of a product or service, and/or because the organization is not customer-driven. *See also* **cost of quality**.

cost of quality. A measurement of what an organization spends for its overall quality. This can be divided into three groups: prevention, appraisal, and failure.

CQI. *See* **continuous quality improvement**.

critical process. Any process that represents a potential for significant risk in areas such as safety, health, environment, customer satisfaction, and resources management.

Crosby, Philip B. Known for his concepts of Do It Right the First Time and Zero Defects, his quality improvement methods are based on the Four Absolutes of Quality Management: conformance to requirements, prevention not appraisal, zero defects, and measurements of the cost of nonconformance. He is also the father of the Fourteen Steps to Quality Improvement.[2]

cross-functional team. A team designed to span functional boundaries to mutually improve performance. These teams are comprised of employees who do not normally interact.

customer. Whether internal or external to an organization, a customer is defined as anyone who receives a product, information, or service from another individual or department. The input of both categories of customer into quality initiatives is critical to the success of an organization's quality program.

customer-driven organization. An organization that continually improves its products and services while considering present and future customer needs (real and perceived), requirements, and expectations in every organization action and planning scenario. These organizations typically request customer feedback, such as through surveys and focus groups, on an ongoing basis and actively integrate these needs into their organizational plan.

customer needs. Perceived or real customer desires that an organization seeks to meet in the features of its products and services.

customer service. Providing assistance that meets or exceeds customer expectations.

CWQC. *See* **company-wide quality control**.

CWQM. *See* **company-wide quality control**.

Deming, W. Edwards. Responsible for introducing the concept of "variance" to the Japanese in the early 1950s. He devised the now famous 14 Points.[3]

The Deming Award. *See* Appendix D: The Quality Awards.

employee involvement. *See* **kaizen**.

empowerment. Giving employees the responsibility, authority, and accountability to cause improvements and changes to happen in the organization within prespecified parameters without prior approval. A leader will not empower employees without first providing proper training and the knowledge necessary for well-founded decision making.

The European Quality Award. *See* Appendix D: The Quality Awards.

external customer. The reason an organization exists, one who is outside the organization and who is affected by its products and services.

facilitator. Normally a neutral party who is trained to facilitate discussion, problem solving, and the progress through the continuous quality improvement steps. Also used in **focus groups**.

The Fifth Discipline (New York: Doubleday/Currency, 1990). A work by Peter Senge, the fifth discipline is "systems thinking," which integrally links the other learning organization disciplines of 1) building a shared vision, 2) ongoing personal mastery, 3) reshaping mental models to the good of the organization, and 4) team learning (thinking), which involves open dialogue and discussion.

Fishbone diagram. *See* **cause-and-effect diagram**.

five W's. The Japanese philosophy of asking "why" of a certain "effect," five different times, to arrive at the cause of the problem.

flowchart. A chart comprised of symbols that is used to designate each step of the process being evaluated. A critical step in the TQM process.

focus group. A method used for obtaining customer feedback. An organization uses it to bring individuals together to share their feelings, ideas, reactions, and so on, toward neutral questions regarding a product or service, new or old, existing or projected. The group is facilitated by someone not directly involved with the product or service (to ensure openness) and one who is skilled in focus group facilitation. Focus groups ideally operate using between 8 and 12 participants, depending on the composition of the group and the need for representation.

force field analysis. A pictorial method used for identifying and displaying driving and restraining forces. Provides a visualization of the forces that affect a situation using a horizontal line with forces pushing from the top and the bottom. Relieving these forces results in process improvement.

freedom to fail. An organizational atmosphere where employees are empowered to make risk decisions without fear of unwarranted repercussions from their boss.

functional work group. A group that is organized around common job functions where employees perform specific tasks and work within a basic hierarchical structure. Rewards are tied to individual performance, and decisions are made up the organizational chain. *See also* **self-directed work team** (for contrast).

Gantt chart. Created by Brian L. Gantt, a bar chart used in project planning for indicating who is going to do what when. It helps plan the schedule, activities, and responsibilities of those involved in the completion of a project. To create this chart, a task list is written down the left side of the chart. A second column (to the right of the task list) is created to indicate the person or persons responsible for the task. Across the top time frames are written such as days, weeks, months, and so on, and vertical lines are drawn down between them to provide divisions. The task start and finish dates are noted by drawing a horizontal line with a symbol (like an arrow or large dot) indicating the end. Assumptions regarding the project are typically indicated to guide the project.

graphs. Pictorial representations of data.

hidden agenda. Refers to a self-serving approach to decision making where decisions or attitudes are based on unrevealed personal goals or objectives. Tends to add negative underpinnings to meetings and difficulty in consensus building.

histogram. A graphic display that shows the shape, spread, and location of a set of data points in order to reveal the amount of variance in a process.

improvement. A change or addition that represents an increase in quality or excellence.

internal customer. The most often forgotten customer component of an organization, internal customers are those who are affected by the products, information, or services of internal suppliers (in other words, the next person in the process chain).

Ishikawa, Kaoru. Responsible for the concepts of company-wide quality, quality circles, and the seven tools used in quality control, such as the cause-and-effect, or Fishbone diagram.

Ishikawa diagram. *See* **cause-and-effect diagram**.

ISO 9000. An international standard which provides a framework for quality by requiring that all procedures and processes be documented. It does not require that the organization improve its quality, merely that it document what it does.

Juran, Joseph. Along with Deming, Juran was influential in shaping the economy of post-war Japan. Developed the Quality Planning Road Map (in which there are nine points) and questioned the effectiveness of quality circles and zero defects strategies. He believed in the quality trilogy of planning, control, and improvement.[4]

just-in-time manufacturing. An approach where the inputs to processes arrive as they are needed by the process for production activities, which effectively maintains a minimal in-process inventory. Draws together the sales, purchasing, and scheduling functions, reducing costs and improving work flow. This system improves quality because problems and waste are not hidden.

kaizen. Japanese term that means continual and gradual improvement by taking well-focused evaluative steps toward higher standards. Can also mean involvement of all employees in organizational problem solving.

leadership. "Leaders communicating clear purpose and vision and enabling and inspiring people to help in achieving that purpose ... provid[ing] a strategy, clear expectations of others, support, personal involvement and resolve and reinforcement of values needed to achieve the purpose."[5]

learning organization. Based on Peter Senge's work, *The Fifth Discipline*, the learning organization bases its culture on generative learning. This style of learning is one that promotes an atmosphere of continuous experimentation and double-loop feedback in an effort to continuously adapt its methods of defining and solving problems. It is an organization that promotes systems thinking, creativity, self-efficacy, and empathy. Adaptability to the changing global markets and the world itself is key to being an effective learning organization.[6]

Malcolm Baldrige National Quality Award (MBNQA). *See* Appendix D: The Quality Awards.

mission. The reason for being of an organization. It links personal and corporate values and is the blueprint by which organizations perform. It is the inextricably linked purpose, values, strategic direction, and standards and behaviors of that organization.

Møller, Klaus. Known for the concept of personal quality as the central focus of TQM, he espouses 12 Golden Rules for Quality Improvement.[7]

nominal group technique. A method for gathering data and for achieving group consensus. *See also* **brainstorming**.

opportunity. A chance for nonconformance to specification. *See also* **six sigma quality**.

paradigm. A pattern, model, or example. Most popular use in the late 1980s and early 1990s is in the phrase "paradigm shift."

Pareto diagram. Provides a quick ranking or order among many different characteristics or facets of an issue. It guides the user to focus on the most important factors in an issue and exhibits that relatively few components account for the bulk of the effect.

Pareto principle. Devised by Kaoru Ishikawa, this principle separates the vital few from the important many. Most commonly known as the 80/20 principle, it seeks to prove that 80 percent of the given population of events comes from 20 percent of the contributors. Also propounded by some as 85/15. An example would be that 80 percent of the books not returned to the library are traceable to about 20 percent of the patrons.[8]

performance improvement team. *See* **quality circle**.

plan-do-check-act (PDCA) cycle. Comprised of four component parts, this process is used as a planning tool for smoothly implementing improvements, planning for meetings and testing, making sure the improvements are on the right track, and so on. It is a systematic approach to problem solving that is useful in any process or activity.

process. A series of interconnected work activities, it is a systematic series of actions designed to meet a specific, planned purpose. Examples of processes in libraries would be hiring new staff, copy cataloging, the reference interview, and performance evaluation.

process control. Systematic review of process performance, including the actions taken in the event of nonconformance.

process improvement. A set of activities designed to detect and remove variation in order to improve process capability.

process performance chart. Developed by Dr. Walter Shewhart of Bell Labs in 1931, it is used to identify changes (or variations) that occur in a process over time. It is also used to study the effect of changes made to the process. The two major components of the control chart are the centerline and the statistical control limits (an upper and a lower line) drawn horizontally. Also know as a **statistical control chart** or just a **control chart.**

product. The output of a process in terms of goods and services. For example, a bound volume, a cataloged set, the catalog itself, the search results from a literature search, an annual report on the department's activities, and so on.

productivity. A measure of production power, it is usually thought of in terms of the ratio of outputs (product) produced to the inputs (what is needed to perform that function).

project improvement team. *See* **quality circle.**

QFD. *See* **quality function deployment.**

quality. Meeting, or exceeding, the customer's perception of both the excellence and/or appropriateness of a product, and the service supporting it. Total quality is achieved by meeting the expectations of our customers, by doing the right thing right the first time, eliminating rework, and by continuously improving and monitoring our processes.

quality action team. *See* **quality circle.**

quality assurance. Assessing the conformance of a product or service to specifications and standards. Establishes a level of confidence in the customer of the quality being offered. This type of assessment is traditionally performed by specialists outside the line operations. This concept recently evolved into the reliability and maintainability of a product or service (accuracy of information, for example) and can result in certification such as BS 5750 or by the Canadian Council of Hospital Accreditation, or simply meeting customer needs.

quality audit. A systematic assessment of an organization's quality program based on a particular standard such as the Malcolm Baldrige Quality Award or other preset criteria. This audit can be performed either internally or as part of the application for a particular award.

quality circle. Invented by Ishikawa, uses the structured data-driven tools of process improvement working within the organization-wide program. In most organizations, it is a team that meets voluntarily (on as frequent a basis as necessary) to improve the quality of a product or service. It includes a sponsor or resource person, leader, facilitator, some include a scribe, and team members. This is a term that, when applied in the United States and the United Kingdom, has taken on an organization-specific definition and now has many names, mostly using the word "team." Synonyms, or quasi-synonyms, include: **quality improvement team, quality improvement project team, project improvement team, TQM team, quality team, continuous quality improvement team, corrective action team, quality action team,** and **performance improvement team.** The major differences occur in the breadth of their responsibility and the composition of the group. What is common in all approaches and definitions is that teamwork and lower-level employee involvement are critical parts of the process and that effective teamwork is critical to the team's success.

quality control. Regulating processes and systems for quality by measuring actual performance, comparing it against standards, and acting on any differences. Success means having a product or service that meets the needs of the customer, is efficiently executed, and is at a reasonable cost.

quality costs. *See* **costs of quality.**

quality council. This is another aspect of TQM that lends itself to a variance of names based on the TQM program of a given organization. The basic definition is a senior management group with the designated responsibility for planning, establishing, managing, and assessing organizational quality and its quality program. Provides direction, sponsorship, and consulting in the quality process. Frequently, in flatter organizations, this council's functions are assigned to the operations management team. Some organizations also call this a **quality steering committee.**

quality function deployment (QFD). A system that employs a method of design based upon the input of all members in the chain, from marketing, designing, engineering, and manufacturing to the customer and supplier.

quality improvement. The sum total of evolutionary and revolutionary beneficial changes that are implemented to increase the level of organizational excellence.

quality improvement project team. *See* **quality circle.**

quality improvement team. *See* **quality circle.**

quality management. The all-inclusive knowledge, methods, skills, and tools used for implementing total quality management as a continuous improvement process.

quality of work life. The overall quality of the workplace for employees. It is the degree to which the organization provides employees with not only a comfortable work environment and the necessary tools to perform their tasks, but also the responsibility, authority, accountability, information, knowledge, recognition, and rewards that enable and encourage them to perform to standards of excellence while they maintain a sense of worth and human dignity.

quality steering committee. *See* **quality council.**

quality team. *See* **quality circle.**

Quality University Environment (QUE). Currently used as the TQM program label at the University of Wisconsin-Madison.

QUE. *See* **Quality University Environment.**

reengineering. "The fundamental rethinking and radical redesign of business processes to achieve dramatic improvements in critical, contemporary measures of performance, such as cost, quality, services, and speed."[9]

root cause analysis. The process of determining the true cause(s) of a problem. Major tools for this analysis are the Pareto chart and the cause-and-effect diagram.

scatter diagram. A graphic presentation to determine if there is a correlation among variables. Also known as a **scattergram.**

self-directed work team. Teams empowered to implement process improvements within specified parameters where the team members are responsible for frontline decision making (i.e., empowered) without having to push the request up the administrative chart. One of the requirements for a successful total quality program, these work groups are ultimately responsible for a discernible end product and are cross trained to cover the entire breadth of the product. They are a permanent fixture in the day-to-day work environment, unlike quality circles. *See also* **quality circle** and **functional work group** (for contrasts).

Senge, Peter. Author of *The Fifth Discipline* and father of the **learning organization.** *See also* ***The Fifth Discipline.***

service. An act of providing assistance or aid to another. Also the support mechanism for a product.

seven quality tools. The basic initial tools were: cause-and-effect diagram, check sheet, control chart (Shewhart), histogram, stratification, Pareto chart, and scatter diagram.[10] There are now the Seven New Tools for Quality Control [11] and GOAL/QPC has designed a program around these new tools calling them The Seven Management and Planning Tools. *The Memory Jogger Plus+*™ illustrates them well.[12]

sigma. A letter in the Greek alphabet (Σ), it is a term that is used to measure the capability of a process to perform at a zero defect level. It is a statistical term that relates to quality.

six sigma quality. A concept based on the term "sigma" which signifies the distribution or spread about the mean of any procedure or process. From a process perspective, it is a metric that defines how well a process is performing. To achieve six sigma value, the process must produce no more than 3.4 defects per million opportunities. An opportunity is defined as a chance for nonconformance to specification.

SPC. *See* **statistical process control**.

special cause. Causes of variation in a product or service due to a unique event and not a commonly occurring incident (common cause). Studied using a **process performance chart**.

spreadsheet. An orderly arrangement designed for planning purposes with the elements of the plan on one axis and resulting responses on the other axis.

SQM. *See* **strategic quality management**.

statistic. Any parameter that can be determined based on the quantitative characteristics of the sample.

statistical process control (SPC). Developed by Shewhart to study the variations in a process over time. It is an equation that is used to construct control charts. *See also* **process performance chart**.

statistical control chart. *See* **process performance chart**.

strategic planning. Process for developing an organization's short and long-term goals usually covering a three- to five-year period and updated at least annually.

strategic quality management (SQM). A process designed to establish strategic goals at the executive level that defines the methods and resources required to reach those goals. (*See* Riggs' reprinted chapter from *Advances in Library Management* [1992] in this sourcebook for more on this topic.)

team building. The process of turning a related group of individuals into a team committed to each other, the team leader, team goals, and the organization.

total quality control (TQC). Coined by Dr. Armand V. Feigenbaum, it is defined as "an effective system for integrating the quality development, quality maintenance, and quality improvement efforts of the various groups in an organization so as to enable production and service at the most economical levels which allow for full customer satisfaction."[13]

total quality management (TQM). Also known as continuous quality improvement, it is a system that introduces and uses customer-driven concepts, processes, and tools, and continuously seeks to measure its success at meeting customer needs and improve upon its processes. It involves total organization participation and customer focus.

TQC. *See* **total quality control**.

TQM team. *See* **quality circle**.

unobtrusive reference study. Evaluation of reference librarians' performances without their prior knowledge.

variable. A data item that assumes values within some range, with a certain frequency or pattern.

variance. In the TQM environment, it signifies any nonconformance to specifications.

variation. The act, process, or accident of varying from a standard over successive operations of a process.

vision. The future view of the organization upon which is based the strategic plan and goals and objectives of an organization. Tends to be expressed in the present tense.

x-bar chart. An average chart.

zero defects. Devised by Philip Crosby, it is a term used to describe a defect-free product.

Notes

1. Kaoru Ishikawa. *What Is Total Quality Control: The Japanese Way.* Translated by David J. Lu. (Englewood Cliffs, N.J.: Prentice-Hall, 1985), 90-91.

2. John Gilbert. *How to Eat an Elephant: A Slice by Slice Guide to Total Quality Management.* (Merseyside, England: Tudor Business Publishing, 1992), 26.

3. Ibid., 21.

4. Ibid., 21-22.

5. *Total Quality Management: Strategies for Local Government. Participant's Handbook.* (Washington, DC: International City/County Management Association, 1993), 121.

6. Michael E. McGill, John W Slocum, and David Lei. "Management Practices in Learning Organizations." *Organizational Dynamics* 21, no. 1 (Summer 1992):5.

7. Gilbert, 27.

8. Ibid., 118.

9. Michael Hammer and James Champy. *Reengineering the Corporation: A Manifesto for Business Revolution.* New York: HarperBusiness, 1993.

10. Ishikawa, 198.

11. Shigeru Mizuno, ed. *Management for Quality Improvement: The Seven New QC Tools.* (Cambridge, Mass.: Productivity Press, 1988).

12. Michael Brassard. *The Memory Jogger Plus+^{TM}: Featuring the Seven Management and Planning Tools.* (Methuen, Mass.: GOAL/QPC, 1989), vii-viii. [*See* Appendix A: Creating an In-House Support Collection for annotation on this work.]

13. Ishikawa, 90.

Index

183